ON OBEDIENCE

ADRIENNE VON SPEYR

On Obedience

Translated by
Robert Van Alstyne, S.J.

IGNATIUS PRESS   SAN FRANCISCO

Original German edition:
Das Buch vom Gehorsam
© 1966 by Johannes Verlag, Einsiedeln

Cover design by Roxanne Mei Lum

© 2024 Ignatius Press, San Francisco
ISBN 978-1-62164-545-0 (PB)
ISBN 978-1-64229-196-4 (eBook)
Library of Congress Control Number 2023944994
Printed in the United States of America ∞

CONTENTS

FOREWORD

This slim volume is one of the last works dictated by Adrienne von Speyr. Like many of her other late texts, it can be taken as an overview of her entire Christian vision—a vision which always sees, as it were, a perfect, rounded whole, where every cross-section captures the complete picture. This is particularly true of *On Obedience*. Its structure is not built from the ground up, stone by stone, nor is it simply deduced from some overarching concept hovering above. Rather, Adrienne contemplates the whole, and even when some single aspect comes to the fore, one can hear this whole resonating together with it.

For her, this whole means both heaven and earth, God and creation. If we speak of the earth and its relations without also speaking of the Lord's heaven—from which this earth arose, toward which it is always striving, and which forever stands open above—we have understood nothing of the earth, or at least nothing of Christian revelation. This whole means the Trinity, Christ, Mary, the

Translated by Thomas Jacobi, Ignatius Press.

Church, and the individual Christian. The chain cannot be broken; the last link cannot be grasped without knowledge of the one that comes before it, then the one before that, and so on, reaching all the way to the mysterious pinnacle of Triune love, which in the concept of *obedience* appears more clearly than ever as the ground and goal of all things. This whole also means paradise, the Fall, the Old Covenant, atonement, redemption. It means the Incarnation, the Cross, Christ's death and descent into hell, the Resurrection and the Ascension, the Spirit and the Church. And the Church means both states of life: lay and consecrated.

So all is ever in all, and we can distinguish each single thing only through a strong awareness of its connection with everything else. Although *On Obedience* does not deal directly with this idea, such an understanding of relation is indispensable to an understanding of identity. Of course, this leads inevitably to dialectical formulations, at least when one is writing about many things that must also be "sublated" (Hegel's term) into larger relationships. So it is, too, with Christian obedience, its limits and limitlessness, its finitude and infinity, according to whether we think of the Christian as a finite creature or as a member of Christ—Christ who "infuses" his own infinite obedience into the believer. Dialectical language is the only kind that is concrete, because it alone accommodates, however incompletely, the "growing together" (Latin: *concrescere*) of God and man, heaven and earth, death and life. Language that divided and excluded would be abstract.

This is of especially decisive importance for the topic of obedience. Christian obedience can only be understood when one sees it as flowing from love and leading toward love—as simultaneously intending and containing love in every single act. Adrienne speaks from within this concreteness, and she does so with a marvelous clarity, precision, and even practicality, not only for our age—which will only overcome its disgust with obedience if it develops a holistic vision—but for all individuals who wish to live out obedience in a deeper way, whether as laymen or as consecrated religious.

All the texts in this volume come from verbal dictations by Adrienne von Speyr. The eleven chapter titles were given by the author herself, while I, the editor, have added the headings.

Hans Urs von Balthasar

What Is Obedience?

Worldly Obedience and Faith

Whoever considers his existence must admit that he cannot control countless things that are laid upon him in a compulsory manner. He is aware of many of these from experience; he has thought about them or run into them. There are many, too, of which he is unaware, but whose reality he acknowledges without giving an account of them and often in complete disinterest. At work he is fixed in his occupation like a link in a chain, and he cannot break this chain—not even bend it. Working hours are determined. Superiors are appointed. A host of appointments must be kept. The pace of work and required performance can be set, or one can only adjust these very slightly. He is also dependent upon his co-workers. If this or that is not provided, he cannot do his own job. If another does not help him, he will not finish. He depends upon materials, upon a thousand circumstances.

If his work interests him, he will want to study the process in which he is involved in order to review the achievement of his predecessors to try to learn what will become of the work he will hand on. Whether one is a handyman or a chemist or an attorney, one seldom starts at a true beginning. Rather, one accepts what others have worked on, which, for him, is only relatively "raw material" that he will further process in order to deliver it reconfigured somewhere else. Often, he will be able to observe the success of his work, but not always. Perhaps he has to spend hours only operating the handle of a machine without seeing what it produces. He must insert himself into an entire process; this can be a burden for him, but he has to live, and existence brought him to the choice either to force himself to do this work or to look elsewhere. So he chose this work—perhaps it was not much of a decision, more a fate laid upon him that hardly waited for personal consent—because it appeared to him reasonably suitable for the existence he has to lead. Still less does he expressly choose to remain there. The fact of his continuing existence simply imposes it upon him. Whether his work appears to him to be useful, whether it suits him—one soon stops asking such questions. He needs the pay, and, besides that, he retains a certain freedom: he can do this just as well as something else. Being tied to the machine, to the work shifts, to the personal relationships of the plant or, if he happens to have a more sophisticated job, to the cases that present themselves to him as a doctor, to the parties he must satisfy as a legal advisor—with all of this he contents himself and always looks forward to so-called free time.

If he thinks about this, however, he will also see a host of dependencies. His environment influences him. Here, too, much more than he thought, he is one who is inserted and who must comply. He can act as though he reigned; at home he can tyrannize his wife, scold the children, and play the part of a great lord. Nevertheless, he must learn to eat the bread that has been purchased, even if today it is too dark and not to his liking; he must bear with the noise of his neighbors, and the more he requests, the more deeply he falls into dependency. Were he a model citizen, he would be the man who does not rebel, but who much rather fits in everywhere, who somehow in his demands keeps pace with advancing technology, who possesses the power of mind to bear everything that weighs him down, bores him, and disturbs him. There he would attain to being a master—everywhere else he is a slave, or his freedom is at least hampered. In this respect, he does not essentially differ from everyone else. He bears this fate together with all. If he buys something that delights him, at the same time he divests himself of certain freedoms—neither acquisition nor wise docility makes him freer. He could most likely still imagine himself to be free in intellectual matters. Probably, no one can keep him from spending an hour a day considering a certain issue, solving a math problem, acquiring some knowledge or even an education. Even here, however, he bumps up constantly against boundaries: unlimited spirit is not available to him. Boundaries are even imposed upon the play of his imagination. He constantly asks himself: "What now? What next?" He might imagine tackling some problem that no one else has faced. He might consider it until he arrives at a unique and definitive solution. He might persevere until he actually reaches this goal, but afterward the emptiness would be there once more, with a thousand further questions that arose along the way to the solution and that now cry out for solutions of their own. It might happen that he then becomes conscious of his own finitude, futility, and transience as never before. Profound discontent and hopelessness can beset him. Perhaps then he remembers the Christian faith.

❋ ❋ ❋

The solution that faith offers him is not a consolation for those who have resigned themselves. It is, rather, a solution unto hope. The obedience that man is compelled to render things does not become less severe for the believer, but the entire drudgery recedes to something secondary. Certainly, one of man's tasks lies in doing his worldly work as it must be done. Faith, however, gives to things and to the work done on them another appearance. My fellowman is no longer first of all one who performs the same drudgery in front of me, next to me, or behind me; he is someone to be loved, someone to whom I must mediate something of what radiates from faith. Wherever my fellowman appears, whether at home, in the workplace, or wherever else, he is not to be missed; love points to him, he poses a question, and this question always finds its reply in the space of faith. He thus appears within a different kind of obedience, one that is already fully penetrated by hope, faith, and the question of love. Christian obedience becomes perpetually relevant through the Lord's commandment to love: one's fellowman is to be loved because he is "neighbor". He must be regarded and considered. As one's fellowman, he is first of all simply present. He does not especially intrude (*drängt sich*)—at least, not usually—or form any urgent (*vordringliche*) matter. The Christian, too, who is supposed to consider him in the commandment to love, does not intrude (*drängt sich*). That which is urgent (*das Drängende*) lies in the commandment itself.

At first, the commandment stands there as something neutral. It is one of Christ's remarks, a word that he spoke to his companions along the way. It is a demand of the most general kind. Whenever Christ speaks, however, he issues a living, effective word that wants to be received and will only then show itself to be what it is: a request for the same obedience as that which the Son renders the Father. Christian obedience would thus be, in a first, most general description, the reception of the Lord's commandment to love, agreement with the one who lives it himself before God, and the adjustment of one's own life to the meaning of love. At first, everything is almost formless. Above all, more love is demanded, and you and I and he, we must love in order to meet this demand.

This demand of the Lord is *the first thing* we encounter *that knows no boundaries*, that is not determined by this or that limit, this or that measure of time, by the laws of workflow and free time, by the choice of some hobby. Rather, it is universally valid, enlists the whole life of man, and indeed, not from the perspective of man's need, but from that of the word of the Lord, which claims one's entire lifetime for this end.

Each human assent to love is like a tiny drop in the sea. Before long, it ceases to be recognized because all of the drops belong to the whole, to a unity that flows forth over the whole world. This unity, however, has its recognizable source in the word of the Lord that he himself speaks in obedience to the Father. Our obedience is the will to be this single drop in the sea—better yet, to be any drop without distinction, without a mark of identification, without recognition. Countless drops are needed in order for this sea to exist. That I am precisely this one drop and have only an indefinite, implicit notion of the others corresponds to the meaning of Christian existence: anonymous obedience that enters into the whole ultimately means, because of the love that the Lord has for each one, *distinguished* obedience, an obedience that is consistent and momentous, expected and demanded to be so by providence.

Love: The One Word

As soon as the commandment to love one's neighbor gains for a man a resonance that he understands and that concerns him, obedience and responsibility also acquire a new appearance. Whoever is addressed must respond and, indeed, not anonymously, but personally and uniquely. This uniqueness of the response becomes pregnant ever anew with responsibilities as well as integrations, opportunities for a further response, and urgency. It also generates something new, insofar as until now some things were known but not heeded. All the new features ultimately derive from the word and the face of the Lord. The features are different, each according to the one who gives the response, and yet they all belong together, and their unity lies in the word and the face of the Lord.

Now the man abandons the neutrality he has maintained until now. He must show his true colors. He is also exposed: dangers arise, for now he is observed and excites offense. Before he was finally willing to obey Jesus' commandment, if he wanted to parse it in advance, to delimit the obligations, to outline obedience, he would thereby design something that has little in common with reality. Reality is always different from the plans to deal with it. Whoever only considers the decision and its possible consequences is still far from being the one who actually bears these consequences. Such a one is in a state of suspension; he does not yet know what will happen. If, in the moment that we recognized Jesus' commandment, we were to envision how to obey it, certain faces from our surroundings would probably emerge. We would undertake to fulfill the commandment toward these people. We would plan the necessary steps and make the arrangements.

But readiness for obedience to the Divine Word requires first of all a complete interior cleaning, an emptiness, an availability, a complete readiness for everything that the Word might work or command. In the moment of decision, what matters is letting everything go, even at the risk of seeing one's entire self disappear, because another world claims us. Everything that until now counted as one's own: the time of work and of rest, for example, the natural rhythm of day and night—all of it is offered up so that the Word can work as it wills and not be limited and compromised by our deficient readiness. If we want to be the measure for the Word ourselves, then there can be no talk of Christian obedience. And we alone would be the truly deficient ones, were we to protect ourselves against the Word of God by setting limits and conditions.

❋ ❋ ❋

Relationships hold sway between man and things and time, and in a certain measure, man has things and time at his command. He must, however, hearing the Word of love, let go even of this last control. There is a listening to the Word into nothingness—into something that, at first glance, has little to do with eternity, but still less to do with the present, because the Word lasts and abides and its perpetuity grounds something that cannot be overlooked. The more man considers this, the more he gets a sense of the way that everything he has until now called his existence consisted purely of things that only had very fleeting worth and then withdrew from his disposal. These included delightful as well as repugnant things and many to which he was indifferent but that were nevertheless there. Everything woven together yielded his existence, that in which he had grown up, that had shaped his life until today. Inside this patchwork there suddenly sounds the command of obedience to love. He who is a thousand times conditioned hears the Word, which is unconditioned, which comes from another world, and he is himself supposed to become that other whom the Word claims. At first, perhaps, he thinks that it will be done with a single listening and obeying and that all the details that surrounded him and constituted his very self are thereby more or less overcome. Perhaps it is precisely this idea that helps him to a first confident Yes. If he then begins to consider his fellowmen from a new perspective, he can make the discovery that those who are reputedly obedient to the Word do not particularly stand out, do not attract attention with any brilliance, so that he has little desire to make their fate his own. He learns some things about their way of life that appear to him hardly worthwhile; he sees, perturbed, that behind their obedience a mystery conceals itself that is no longer traceable. He cannot apply any human measure to it; the measure that is contained in the Word is apparently a measure of God that man can apply neither to himself nor to another.

He also does not quite know how to carry it out in order to follow the one Word. Until now he has obeyed a thousand words, at times orienting himself toward one word, and then toward the other; now that he prepares himself to obey the *one*

Word, he does not see how one does it. Once he gathers his courage together and attempts it anyway, he discovers, amazed: this Word is so alive that it has the power in itself to make the agent capable. It is the Word that asserts itself and unfolds itself within him. When he has grasped this, it also becomes clear to him that human "self-realization" is an empty word. By the inner power, speed, and steadfastness with which the Word of love unfolds itself, he recognizes that alone this Word has the power to assert itself in man. It is not as though it would spread through a kind of contagion, but rather the fullness of the Word fulfills itself in man.

The Church

"It is no longer I who live; Christ lives in me": Paul's word expresses a truth that applies to each Christian. It is not, however, as though everyone individually must offer himself to the Lord as a dwelling and would thereby have done enough. Nor is it that everyone stands under the same law of the love of neighbor as his fellow Christian, whose openness to the Lord nevertheless does not concern him because he must himself be thankful to some extent if he is to become a dwelling for God. It is much rather that if the Lord dwells in Paul, this man represents the *Church* instituted by Christ. The Church is not only a frame for the individual parts of the enframed picture, which only remain together as long as the frame contains them; as an institution founded by the Lord, she is also herself an image that accepts the believers, integrating them into herself, and she takes into account their particular colors, lights, and shades. She administers the Word of God and the sacraments, from which the individual lives in his innermost [depth]. She poses many questions to him that he has to answer, but one can just as well say that the individual poses the Church many questions that only she can validly answer for him. She lets the Spirit blow through her and continuously receives him in order to give him away and be formed and unfolded by him. And because she receives the Spirit immediately, and the truth is given to her for administration, she demands obedience and discipleship, allocates to each one his place according to his ecclesial gifts of the Spirit, which she administers and whose measure lies with her. And this place that is assigned is no resting place but, rather, a place within an order of obedience, within a hierarchy, on a plain far above the individual. Because the Spirit blows through the Church, vivifying her, this plain is never fixed and dead but, rather, is a source that bubbles over with life. The Church as an institution is herself configured to the Trinitarian God in a relationship of obedience; even the highest office-bearer cannot suddenly will to believe things or will to let things be believed that do not stand within God's living plan for the Church. The "little man", who believes but possesses little understanding, will perhaps never feel the moment of obedience to the Church very strongly. He will fulfill the duties demanded of him naturally and without questions; he will keep his Easter and receive the various sacraments at the appointed time without asking much because he simply adheres to the Church's answer to his question about what he should do. His fellow Christian's example will help him insert himself into the current of the tradition before and after him. He would be astounded perhaps if one were to describe his attitude as obedience. Nevertheless, he obeys, as do the others. Here and there he does so grumpily, but without serious rebellion. He demands for himself no special law; he does what the others do, too.

One who is spiritually more alert, one who has been formed, will likely consider some of this ecclesial conduct to be genuine obedience, since it awakens unresolved questions within him. He will not always be able to understand fully why something that he wishes to be different is not possible and he has to yield. But the Church also possesses answers for him, more differentiated answers in which the inquirer, if he is attentive, will sense the blowing of the Spirit more clearly and will feel the Spirit blown upon himself. He renders a more conscious obedience, absorbs more consciously first what the Church says, and he holds it to be true, and only then will he raise his objections and, in the response he receives, experience the ever deeper insight of the Church. Thus will he also appreciate better the legitimacy of the demand of obedience and the extent of its claim. He will further understand that an order must govern the community; he will also see the priest as one of those obeying within a hierarchical order, which can never exist otherwise than through the fulfillment of obedience. The order of the Church now appears as an organism of obedience, wherein one has to fulfill this and another that in the space that has been outlined, but this whole obedience is a spiritual one, whose meaning reaches much deeper than one initially thought. It therefore also imposes a greater responsibility, all the more so, the more awake is the faith that senses how subtly the effects of Christian actions branch out in every direction. The whole activity reaches out toward the Head of the Church, who performs the whole obedience to the Father and recapitulates it in himself, without the believer being able to picture very much to himself by this truth. Obedience fastens into obedience; something set fits into something else that has been set. Thus it runs to the exterior of rites, which structure the liturgies and the sacraments, to the formulation of the dogmas that establish the faith and make it into a clearly felt act of obedience. Obedience of the individual mind to the Church, of the mind within the Church, of the Church to the Lord, of the Lord to the Father. From the outermost leaf to the deepest root, the tree forms a whole that lets itself be understood as a unity most clearly in terms of obedience, of the Son's will to obey, which he granted to his Church. *Extra Ecclesiam nulla salus*: salvation embodies itself in the Church because only in the Church is there real obedience.

As the unbeliever, in his freedom, which he wishes to manage by himself, sees himself unexpectedly placed before new boundaries and forms of obedience, so the Christian finds himself in the Church with thoughts that have nothing directly to do with the Church, and yet always unexpectedly again in the field of an outlined ecclesial obedience. There is no evasion—such a thing is never intended. Since God the Father created all things unto the Son, they all already contain preliminary traces of obedience, which the Son, at the Incarnation, elucidated in the Church. Through the Church, he has imparted clearer and more easily graspable outlines to the whole obedience.

The Christian has in the Church enough of a motive to insert himself into obedience. Sometimes this obedience, viewed from the outside, can be difficult for him. But prayer, the gaze toward Christ, the will to follow him—these help to overcome the obstacles. If he believes it to be true that he no longer lives but Christ lives in him, he only needs to let this word become true in himself in order for obedience also to live in him. This holds even for the times when he discovers all kinds of failures in the Church and feels impaired as a believer, for obedience is for him a power that cleanses and strengthens him, drives him to loftier actions, empowers him to hope anew. Some things in the Church he cannot change, but there are also areas where new things may be discovered and built. Until now, many things were hidden, and they come forward at the appointed time efficaciously. New guidelines and the proclamation of a new dogma are always a witness that the vitality of the Church has not died away; and if she includes in her demand for obedience a new aspect of the truth, then this is likewise a sign of her constant liveliness (and not of her ossification), the co-execution of which she entrusts to the believer—all the more so as the new lies asleep in the old and in that respect was already implicitly affirmed. There is the silence of the Church; there is also her speaking. At certain times, her speaking breaks through her fruitful silence, in order to show what in her silence has ripened: this fruit ought to be accepted with joy by the believer's new and, indeed, old obedience.

2

The Meaning of Obedience

Levels of Obedience

Everything the Word of God ever required of men
had its meaning in Christ. Already with the call to
obedience in paradise, God wanted to keep the first
men within a certain course, at a height already
sketched out, in a readiness that was required in
order to endure continually the presence of God.
God approached them in paradise and withdrew
again according to a rhythm that he alone determined and that, as long as man was obedient, raised
no questions and caused no disturbance. Everything
was good. God himself had judged his work to be
so. This goodness was taken up and confirmed by
men. He lived and moved in this goodness, and this
movement was obedience.

Sin expelled men out of the paradisal goodness;
since then, obedience no longer coincides for him
with that which is self-evident. It became onerous
and confining, training him tediously. It demanded

something from man that ran contrary to him and cost him something. Not without pain, the sinner had to adapt himself to something that was supposed to allow him to live—to what is, admittedly, a hard life of work, penance, and atonement. The ever-new sin perpetually aggravated the difficulty of obedience.

For contemporary man, the urgent issues and demands of obedience arise incessantly and, indeed, usually in such a way that he must say yes to a new constraint, must opt for a tighter bond where he would rather be free and would like to arrange things himself. He can meet the many, ever-increasing demands of obedience that worldly existence brings by integrating himself and possessing enough spiritual freedom to perceive this integration, to bear it, and to profit from it as a school of self-control. In hindsight, he can determine that through such obedience he profited for himself or for others. As soon as the question of others arises, he can see that his obedience eases life for them, allows them to enjoy more freedom, that thus his own maturation and ripening possess for them a significance of brotherhood and love. One sees more easily the formative fruit of obedience in others than in oneself. He can also ascertain, on the other hand, that the obediential integration of his fellowman benefits him, that thus through common obedience an exchange becomes possible, if not exactly of love, certainly for the good, of reciprocal understanding and help. Integration is a social obligation.

With the turn to what is particularly Christian, obedience receives salvific meaning for men. It attains a power and promise unto eternal life, but also a power for the present Church, for her continued existence and life. One can observe and ascertain very well the blessing of obedience in the ecclesial hierarchy, but also in simply belonging to the Church. It is man's reply to the Lord's foundation. The foundation possesses, as institution, the ability to demand this human reply, to receive it and lead it properly. It is, through the Church, man's reply to the Lord: the readiness to take refuge in his Word without ever measuring it by his own experience of grace. This grace lives in obedience; it lives first of all in its own sphere, which is the Lord's sphere; there it steadfastly continues. And man lets it be there. He learns obedience as the small child learns to obey his parents, by letting the words and reasons and insights of the parents be in them. Sometimes the insight even reaches the child, for example, as the consequence of a (perhaps bitter) experience: the candle burns! The stone is hard! Such experiences strengthen the child even further to believe the adults about what they have not experienced. An adult's obedience to the Church consists of a similar mixture of ignorance and experience, which slowly shifts to a mixture of understanding and experience. In the beginning, he grasps as little as the small child; then comes understanding and, with this, joy: joy that he may be there, that he is considered, that he can answer, come nearer to God, and that he can do so precisely by obeying. For each man who is aware of it, obedience will contain some understanding and some not-yet-understanding, which, however, does not diminish the joy. The not-yet-understanding is a form of hope. Something is fulfilled that was almost wordlessly promised, something that belongs to the mysteries of the Church and of the Lord at the same time, and it leads the obeying Christian into the intimacy of these mysteries. It leads him therein, not only because it is something fitting and good for him to do, but rather just as much because it is something the Lord needs, because the Lord wants to be a co-worker, and, in redeeming, he requisitions the redeemed for help with his work of redemption. The whole intelligibility of the will of Christ unfolds itself in this obedience of the believer, reflects and reveals itself in it, shows him the way, accompanies him, and draws him ever more intimately into a common obedience.

Ultimately, obedience also has meaning for the whole world, for Christ's obedience and his work of redemption are intended for the world as a whole, which is to be brought back to the Father. Thus, no act of obdience to the Son is lost; he gathers them all in and gives them the true fullness of meaning. Approving, agreeing, completing, he gathers every attempt and bundles them into a sheaf. He gives maturity to every act of obedience; indeed, he ultimately gives to those obeying the meaning of obedience altogether. If everything is created for him, then every worldly obedience is also oriented toward the hidden Trinitarian meaning of obedience. Whoever may obey is invited by the Son to participate in his intimacy with the Father and the Spirit. If an experienced, older Christian were to tell of his life in the Lord, of the effects of his faith in his existence, he would certainly (even if not necessarily explicitly) outline a way of obedience, and one would see: wherever something great and joyful happened in his life, it was an event and a radiating of obedience. Only the No, the refusal, is sterile. This blocks the light that would have illumined and warmed. Every Yes, on the other hand, even the most tentative, lets light in and lets a seed grow up, today or perhaps much later, here or even somewhere else entirely. Obedience is always an act of hope into love, grounded by faith and so born that in obedience faith becomes a new faith, weaker faith becomes strong faith, and human faith becomes that which is communicated in grace by the covenant between the Father and the Son in the Holy Spirit. Through obedience, man is taken into this exchange, which by the Son's earthly obedience is mediated to his redemption of the world. And this plan has existed from the foundation of the world and gives to all things in the world and Church their ultimate meaning.

Formation toward the Center

Listening carefully to the Word of God, the Christian is met by the Word in that place of his spirit where he is accustomed to pose questions and responses, to give an account, to conceive resolutions, to set upon actions. God speaks to him in such a way that he really perceives his voice and knows what is meant. God has as Creator the power to make himself intelligible to his creature; he has given to his creature in turn the power to understand his voice and to be able to align himself accordingly.

Obedience thus at first means something generally human for the Christian; he is not alone; countless others also respond to God before him, after him, beside him. He understands better than others, however, that his response binds him ever more closely to God, because in faith each assent has its consequence. Each act of obedience is like a shell, which, once used and discarded, exposes a new shell—until everything is used up. That is to say, until God really occupies every place in the believer. This will require waging battle. Obedience wants renunciation, purification, purity. And the person obeying learns, the more he obeys, that he is not yet transparent enough, that he still withholds much that he must surrender. He can also be sullen; but a sulky obedience is no obedience. God wants his own to know joy. Each of the Lord's renunciations in suffering occurs for the sake of redemption and for the sake of joy as it breaks out at Easter. And also, to those whom he calls very near to his Cross, he never gives suffering as that which he himself has endured. He allows them to taste it, but out of grace, and his ultimate intention is always joy. This lies hidden in Christian obedience. If two people who love each other, each animated with his own wish, are unable to fulfill both wishes at the same time, then each will desire to renounce his own wish out of love for and joy in the other, in order to fulfill the other's wish. This renunciation will be one of love and will have joy for its driving force. Neither of the two will want even to utter the word renunciation. So must every Christian adoption of obedience be joy in the Easter joy of the Lord. A joy that would like to hold everything the Lord wants to put into it. It is like a great vessel of joy, even if in this vessel there occurs some suffering, some renunciation, some awaiting, some apprehension.

Seen thus, obedience would be an education into joy. It is at the same time an education into eternity. A first step approaching eternal life, where everything is so much joy that even what here below we name obedience will there bear only the name of joy. The Church is not called the Bride of the Lord for nothing: the Bridegroom rejoices in his Bride; he desires, however, that the Bride also rejoice in him. And every ecclesial obedience, that which is felt as a heavy burden, as well as that which is hardly noticed, that which is contained in the confession of faith as well as that which is mediated in the sacraments:[1] each belongs to this bridal joy. And the Church's liturgical year, which celebrates so many saints, presents the Lord's obedience next to her own obedience for imitation and shows, already through the feast, that joy is thereby intended. Whatever saints we celebrate—Mary Magdalen or John the Baptist or an apostle or a founder—we always celebrate in a distinguished manner the special way in which the saint obeyed God. How much more is this the case for the feasts of the Mother of God and those of the Lord.

And because the Church is a bride who finds her center and embodiment in Mary, the Church in her special ecclesial obedience points clearly to Mary's obedience to the angel, to the Holy Spirit, to the Son, to the whole Triune God. It is an obedience that is performed in joy and remains in it and spends

---

[1] In each Communion, for example, something of the obedience of the Lord is given, but also something of the obedience of all.

it. Already her words, "let it be done unto me ..."
exude the joy of a completely fulfilled obedience.
Because she says Yes, the Son becomes man. Her
participation in the Incarnation initially consists
solely in her obedience, her silent integration. And
because her obedience is there, everything else is
already included. And in this center everything
is gathered, from her election before all time up to
her assumption into heaven, together with everything that her destiny on earth as the Mother of
the Lord will be. She lets everything happen, and
in the middle of it all, she acts.

Every Christian obedience weaves itself together
from both a letting-happen and a doing: no Christian obedience is purely active; none is purely passive. These two encounter each other, penetrate
each other, and the proximity becomes invisible,
just as an invisible proximity also unites obedience
and joy. The meaning of obedience, therefore, is
convergence, assimilation, and the examples of this
that the Church gives us and that permeate the
whole history of salvation are so numerous that no
man will ever know them all, will ever be able to
imitate them all. But every Christian can fit himself
to this chain as a pearl; he can place his life under
the sign of obedience in general, and yet do so in
such a way that it does not lose itself in "vagueness"
but, rather, always even precisely, clearly, singularly
penetrates his doing and letting.

The Effects of Obedience

Where a man plans something himself, he can to a large extent determine the measure of his commitment, even the course of the business he has undertaken. From his plan, he can let further plans unfold for the future into a general program of life. It can also happen, however, that he undertakes his program of life in obedience. Obedience will possibly lay upon him the same tasks and duties that he had undertaken himself. His position has thus doubled: on the one hand, he must perform the work undertaken in obedience as perfectly as possible, as though it were his own plan; he must apportion time and means corresponding to his powers, as would apply if in everything he were completing his own work. Alongside this complete dedication, however, there is his readiness to renounce it all, not as a contrary, but running along with the dedication; he is ready to renounce it all in case obedience should demand something else of him. Thus, he will do with utmost exertion what he might also at any moment relinquish to another, something that perhaps, though it appears to him meaningful and fruitful, does not please the person charging him with his task. Here, complete dedication and complete availability stand beside one another: love for the task as for something personal and letting it go out of a still greater love.

We can hardly grasp such an attitude with the understanding. For how, outside of obedience, should one be able to comprehend that he squanders his best powers on one task and has agreed at the outset to attribute to this act no ultimate meaning—that one undertakes an important task and remains ready to exchange it with one that is (in the judgment of the world) entirely trivial? And yet both, dedication and readiness, must be carried out earnestly. Thus the full Yes to the task already contains a possible No to the same task; both the Yes and the No, as powers, are immanent in obedience, not contrary to one another. They do not cancel each other out or destroy each other but, rather, reciprocally fructify each other. For the No to the task is the expression of a stronger Yes to obedience. This is admittedly only possible in living faith, where everything, the Yes and the potential No, issues within its sphere and thereby avoids the usual considerations. For a man who lacked faith would execute complete dedication only for *one* task, which appeared to him assured. Were the task revoked from him for some reason, his zeal would wane; he would separate himself from it very reluctantly and attempt at least at a distance to pursue it further. But even he would have to gather his strength anew and seek another task that appeared to him worth full dedication.

The inclusive No of the believer, however, is no betrayal of the importance of the task, no contempt for the striving that one has undertaken up to this point. It much rather arises from an abundant readiness for every possible new Yes, for every possible new task, which again will imply a No of the same readiness. This is obedience without grumbling and knowing better.

Periods of human work have a duration that is not entirely to be foreseen; God should be able to have this duration at his command; man leaves his work to the discretion of God, who also assesses its worth. He serves God in such a way that he does not determine ahead of time his desires, not even the desirability of his desires, but rather he only ever does what God commands. This can produce a zig-zag line; but it can also bring about one that, when seen from the result of the work, is nice and straight. For the person who obeys, this in itself makes no difference. For his life's meaning lies in God's hands. He will only try again and again to do what is demanded of him as well as possible. He will not, ahead of time, consider how long it will take and what the outcome will be. There is in every obedience a *return* of time. It could definitely happen that one who is gifted and who works successfully must give up an important task in favor of an unimportant one. Value is thus suspended. The one commanding presides in judgment over it. The person obeying, however, learns to shift his mind, his assessment of the things he apprehends. He learns to surrender it. He renounces it. He does this in the place where the Lord says, "Not my will". The Son does not argue with the Father. The Father knows, however, what the will of the Son is and what his own will is.

Surrendering a work has two aspects: that of renouncing the task previously undertaken and that of undertaking the new task. In obedience, the two do not conflict. If someone in the world undertakes something new, he will weigh the advantages and the disadvantages and make his decision depending upon many aspects. The one who obeys cannot make this decision. He will perhaps talk about the change and discuss the reasons as they appear to him. But such reasons may never be that he desires to grow with the challenge or that he is sure, as the only one appointed and suitable for this task, to be thus somehow indispensable. It is difficult in such situations to learn to obey, but the readiness must be summoned. If a Christian knows that God demands from him an act of obedience, he will thus be able to complete it in peace and ultimately in joy. In order to be able to do this, he must attach more weight to readiness than to his accomplishment. And even this he cannot do in virtue of his own discretion and calculation, but rather in the commitment that the joy has in itself. As the Son was *gladly* ready to become man and take the Cross upon himself, so will the Christian learn, from his readiness, to summon up joy, because he may choose the greater good and receive a share in the joy of the Lord. Between the acting and the readiness, no gap may open; between the Yes and the No, there may be no empty place. Again, something seamless is required. There is thus no point of neutrality where I consider that I could undertake task A just as well as task B; rather there is, because of the seamlessness, only the pure leap from task A into task B. I have given everything for task A, and I will likewise give everything for task B; no complicated transition is necessary; a framework does not need first to be taken down for a long time and another set up.

Expansion by Obedience

Obedience to God enlarges the world of man by drawing things into the realm of the possible that it had not occurred to him to consider. He has to confront the difficulties that such a sudden expansion contains in itself. In some circumstances, he must suddenly bear before his surrounding world the responsibility for things for which, until now, another—God, the Church, the Superior—bore the responsibility. Joys could also thereby come to him of which he knew nothing. He must insert himself into the newly fashioned environment as the person he is. His boundaries have shifted, and perhaps it is not only an imperceptible shift: where previously he had a wall before his eyes, suddenly there can stretch a broad field, a spiritual world, which it is from now on necessary to master. Or he had finally renounced certain things that suddenly stand before him again as a task. Thus, there is also here again a No and a Yes; one had spoken the No out of personal, ascetical reasons, and now a Yes in joy is supposed to come from it once more. In his readiness, the man has remained the same, only the circumstances around him have fundamentally changed.

The person who obeys is often like a man who has wandered in a restricted region off a path well known to him. He feels himself suddenly lost in a foreign environment in which he at first sees absolutely no way forward. But where God demands authentic obedience, certain things are as though covered; it is likewise with one's own inadequacy: the lack of talent for an area, the lack of courage. It is almost as though God were obliged at the fresh demand of obedience also to equip men with the properties and character traits necessary for the task, with characteristics that the Incarnate Son actually makes available for obedience, so that they, along with doctrine, find their ground in him and stretch out their roots. For obedience does not only change the activity of a man, it also reaches thoroughly into his character, his opinions, his world view. Above all, the whole of revelation, Holy Scripture, contains for the person who obeys a new, much deeper, and more central meaning. He sees now what the words *want to say*. It is not the least meaning of obedience that it sharpens the intuition for the sense of the Lord and his Church so that where previously there was only a fabric of words, suddenly a whole world of meaning can open up.

And the more obedient man is, the more his own I disappears in favor of the "thing", and the thing is the redemption of the world by the love of God on the Cross; the thing is the apostolate, the continuing influence of the Lord in the Church and world. Before obedience became reality, there was universal satisfaction, a standing still on the border. Afterward, the boundaries are gone; today, the Word of God, living, taking hold, lays claim to every space.

The obedient person can, fully conscious of his ability, perform things that he previously never would have been able to or would have wanted to assume, because now his ability lies in God and God entrusts it to him, and because he will not presume to have more knowledge about himself than the superior has. Psychological barriers thus fall away, and one gets a sense of what the Gospel passage about moving mountains means. This can take place if the person's whole power over everything in him is surrendered to the Word.

The child to whom one gives permissions and prohibitions trusts that his parents desire the good. He trusts without reservations in the back of his mind and without reflection. This childlikeness is what God demands of the one who obeys, but while demanding, he also gives it to him. The Spirit of childlikeness therefore finds a true home in the docile person. The person outside of obedience has many theories about what he can do and what he can expect of himself in the most extreme situation. If he becomes obedient, these theories melt away like snow. He sees how things that he previously "did not tolerate" become beneficial for him; in the infinitely broadened space, there is no more space for his old narrow opinion.

One should also consider that the person who exercises Christian obedience is never alone; he is to a special degree the object of the prayer of the Church and of fellow Christians. He can count on their help in God. He will never know how much he is carried; he will never know everything that is averted by prayer, everything that is caused, everything that is lightened; but it is certainly more than he thinks. The person without obedience is not only tied to boundaries, he must generate them himself in order to have the possibility of existing. The person who submits, on the other hand, gives to obedience itself the meaning of a new world, so that obedience means for him what he means for obedience: between both there exists a reciprocity, something that at the same time strengthens the power of obedience and by which, again, the power of the person obeying is increased. An osmosis takes place that escapes every psychological calculation, a most intimate and effective exchange in deep seclusion. Once set in place, the person obeying would be a link in a chain: he performs something that others before him have done and that others after him will again do; thus he does not feel how busy he is to be a limitation. He touches the cramped site of his work from the expanse of his readiness to obey. The work must be done by him or by another; he has been chosen for it; and so this is right. He has the certainty that his path runs straight forward; his deed is true; he has the joy of sharing in every word of assent that is spoken at some time in the Church.

3

The Obedience of Christ

The Incarnation as Obedience

The birth of the Lord is surrounded by sheer mysteries: the mystery of the assenting Virgin Mary, the mystery of the fruitfulness of the unfruitful Elizabeth, the mystery of the obeying shepherds and kings, the mystery of the constellation of many promises that are fulfilled in this birth and that are like footprints into which the Lord places his foot in order to effect fulfillment.

The act of fulfilling set promises is an activity of utmost obedience. The Lord lets his life be determined by the promises in external occurrences, and still much more with respect to his interior attitude. Lines run across the ages connecting the demands to him, and the moment that the promise was spoken touches him so vividly that the temporal distance does not at all mitigate it. It is as though time melts together and runs away, so precisely do promise and

fulfillment fit together, so exactly are the walls of
the New Covenant erected upon the foundation
of the Old.

But the Son does not obey merely a predetermined plan—he obeys personally the personal
Father; he has come for this purpose: to place his
divinity and humanity at the Father's disposal and
to fulfill in all things the Father's will. If the Virgin
is foretold, she would, in deference to the Word,
overshadowed by the Spirit, and as the last consequence of the let-it-be that she uttered before the
Triune God, have to, be permitted to, and want
to bear a Son; in that case, these are such spectac-
ular acts of obedience that they, as signs of a super-
natural obedience—commanded by God, accepted
by men—point to something much greater, something incommensurable: to the act of obedience
that the Incarnation and birth of the Son itself is, a
divine act of obedience for which Mary's obedience
only offers itself as a vessel. Her obedience is fulfilled by his, which includes, determines, generates,
and gives birth to hers. Her obedience is elevated
because the Son of God humbles himself to become
the servant of God. One can say: his divine obedience is humbled into a purely human obedience;
and with this, the obedience of Mary is elevated
beyond everything purely human by the Spirit that
overshadows her—actually beyond what one names
super-natural into a height that only first becomes

apparent at her immediate bodily assumption into heaven. But all of this is a *function* of the obedient self-humbling of the Son.

During the long years in Nazareth as a child, a teenager, and a young man, he is subordinate to her; he places his obedience under her obedience, as her obedience is more deeply placed under his. In this way, he brings about something completely seamless. If she, as the knowing Mother, teaches something to him, the little child, even though he is yet God and knows everything, it becomes impossible to find the seam of obedience, to trace the articulations of this obedience. It is something as singular and as perfectly unified as the Son unifies in himself the unity of God and man. One can say of certain things: these he does primarily as God or primarily as man, but ultimately everything radiates so greatly in his mystery that in most cases differentiating becomes completely impossible. Thus is it also with his obedience to his parents. Knowing who he is, they follow him by raising him to follow. It is already their obedience to him, if they raise him so, as the children of others are raised. And if he at twelve years old in the Temple suddenly gives explanations and does things that are his Father's in heaven, then he does so, not out of disobedience, but rather in order to reveal the deeper source of his obedience. He does so, not in order to release himself from obedience to his parents—he will still be subordinate to them—but rather in order to show them by this example how strongly obedience binds him. And since they do not understand what he says, they are also bound by a tighter obedience, to which he for his part is obedient in turn, as in a fresh lowering of his divine obedience into a human obedience. His obedience to the Father, who understands, is humbled into an obedience to the parents, who do not understand.

His obedience is part of his essence and is fulfilled by him in the way the Father wishes; it is fulfilled by him in Mary and Joseph likewise in the way the Father wishes. It is an obedience of divine Origin that becomes obedience in daily life, giving meaning to daily life and bringing us closer to God through discipleship, and even already through his contemplation. By the Son's obedience, we try to learn what Christian obedience is, because he shows it to us so effusively that we cannot help but absorb something of it. He not only shows it; he gives it. He gives it not only on the Cross, but his whole life long, in every act, constantly.

If, then, the Son leaves home and crowns his contemplative years with his active life, he points continually to the Father. He speaks of him in order to reveal him to men, but also to show how *he* stands by the Father, how truly he is the Son; but to be the Son where the Father is named is an expression of a fully affirmed obedience.

Life in Obedience

In most of the Lord's words, one can recognize obedience: whether he is speaking of the Father and unveiling his relationship to him, or whether he is interpreting Christian truth to men. In all of this, there is the sphere in which he speaks in such a way that the listeners understand exactly what is meant, but also the sphere in which the Word, as it were, resounds in the depths of God and unveils the background of Christ's mind and therewith the background of the mind of the Triune God. The closed coherence of the Word can effect every opening to God.

This holds above all for the Lord's statements about himself. When he says, "I am the way", this does not mean *a* way, but rather the only way to the Father, the way of truth and of life. One cannot hear such a single expression without immediately seeing the whole. "I am the truth" means: the one, necessary truth, enclosing all other truths—thus, present and eternal life are one in him. And precisely in these statements about himself, obedience always becomes visible, too. If he is the way, then he has *become* the way once and for all by the Father's mandate; he also *remains* the way, for he desires to lead through himself to the Father once and for all, and he wants to make his gift to the Father permanent. If he is the truth, then he will never seek another truth than that which he is in obedience to the Father; indeed, it *is* his obedience that he is the truth. Therefore, all the words that he speaks about himself are truths of obedience. The Father hears them, and the Son attests to him of his love by speaking these words of obedience. Each word directed to men is at the same time addressed to the Father and is obedient to him. Each word lies in the place where the Father receives the obedience of the Son, accommodating it in order to find the Son obedient. And when the Son has made the decision to become man, he does so in an obedience that he never betrays his whole life long, but constantly fulfills, and that he gives exactly that form which the Father expects. He does not assure the Father over and over again that he would like to obey him but, rather, testifies to this desire in each of his actions, of which his continual contemplation of the Father is also one. That he never removes himself from the vision—this is obedience. It is natural for him that his obedience in action corresponds exactly to his obedience in spirit. And his obedience of the thirty years is the same as his obedience of the three years.

Moreover, there is a special, continual obedience that he performs by renouncing the knowledge of the Hour. He has so left the Hour to the Father's discretion that he does not peek, does not reveal to himself the point in time. He wants to keep his human readiness always alive, the readiness for obedience unto death. He does nothing in order to move this death nearer or farther; with respect to it, he wants to have no other attitude than that which the Father gives him. The Triune Divine Love is so great that if the Son would, as man, determine the Hour himself, the Divine Father would certainly agree with him. But because the Son, as man, only wants to be the reflection of this Divine Love, without compromise he chooses unknowing. He desires only what the Father desires.

Thus, he naturally also left the hour of the Mother's overshadowing to the Father's determination. He who pre-redeemed Mary certainly knows that she will be his Mother, but as he gives his hour of death to the Father, so too he gives him the hour of his conception. His desire not to know the Hour elevates his gift, because he must render complete readiness without any special preparation for it. He must be completely prepared at every moment; he must make all his strength available for the moment and its demands. And then, if suffering overcomes him, it likewise finds his undivided readiness, and he suffers completely out of complete obedience. The words from the Cross ring out as the expression of the fullness of suffering. They were not rehearsed beforehand but are words that arise ever-presently from the ever-present encounter of an undivided readiness and an indivisible suffering. In this way, they are the pure verbalizations of his obedience of suffering.

And if the Son preaches the doctrine of the Trinitarian God among men in a language man can understand, the choice of words and images is also an act of his obedience. Each expression is at the same time dedicated to men and to the Father. He does not cut back on either relationship. He takes care that every expression sounds and comes across just as true to the Father as to men. He speaks in the Holy Spirit. If he says simple things to men, which do not come to them completely unexpectedly, his words are yet ever laden with everything that they could not expect, everything whose ultimate depth they are not at all permitted to understand because it is the truth of eternal life and only eternity will introduce them to it. His speech is completely simple but saturated by the Holy Spirit. Men understand—and yet do not understand, for how could they grasp the Son of Man's obedience to the Father, the strength of the bond that speaks even from his simplest words. There lies in every word the whole sum of Christian doctrine for him who can hear it. The perfection of his relationship to the Father, the invitation to men to enter into this relationship. The meal to which he calls them again and again is the meal that he takes with the Father, at which he stands before the Father in the obedience of love and desires to know no other world than that of the Father. Proclaiming the Beatitudes, he imparts to men—a great gift!—access to the holiness that he tastes in the unity with the Father. He shows to them the fruit of obedience, whose archetype he himself always is.

He will not voice Paul's expression "imitate me" in the same way because everything he has to say he speaks in the Father. And Paul is to be imitated because he is a man; Christ is not to be imitated, because he is God. Only at a distance can we lag behind along the way that he is. He is only imitable as the inimitable one. Sure, he has become man in order to give us a share in his divine sphere. But even amid its communication, this sphere remains a mystery; it is his intimate sphere, the sphere of his absolute love for the Father in which he is absolutely, divinely obedient to the Father. Something of this sphere is perceptible also in each of his human acts of obedience. The integration of his human will into the Father's will is, in the Son himself, in communion with his divine integration. Therefore, by participating in the mystery of Christ and in his obedience, we inevitably come to the point where his inimitable character becomes visible for us.

Miracle and Cross as Obedience

God gave the created world laws; he gave them to individual creatures and also to men; he has regulated their relationships according to laws, and likewise has he regulated the course of time. Man can penetrate more deeply into these laws; he can draw on them extensively, but only if he recognizes them and obeys them in some way. Whether he knows them or not, he lives in them, and their validity for the world is a consolation for him. In general, he would find it troublesome if this validity were somehow broken. The same is true if one of his fellowmen behaves conspicuously otherwise and so appears to follow foreign legalities. The question suddenly arises: Why is he doing this? One is only reassured again if an answer emerges from the laws that have up to this point been valid.

Christ works miracles. He not only does striking things, he does things that burst the normative character of every worldly law. He multiplies bread and fish so abundantly that not only are thousands satisfied, but much more remains left over than was initially there. He can do such things only from a power that lies beyond all worldly law and communicates itself to worldly things, like bread and fish. The miracles worked, however, are only a means for the Lord, a sign to make men attentive to the Father and to indicate to them at the same time his own relationship to the Father. It is not the Father who obeys him when the Father works a miracle through him, the Son of Man; rather, the Son obeys the Father by employing for the Father's glorification what the Father makes available to him, what he is capable of doing through the Father. It is a demand of his obedience that redeems the world in the name of the Father and for him.

There are miracles through which his position becomes completely clear. He calls Lazarus back from the grave, thus letting his voice ring out in the realm of the dead. Lazarus answers by coming back to life. The Lord works the miracle so that the Father may be glorified and by thanking the Father for it. In this act of obedience of the Son, one sees that the law of death, which was laid upon men as a punishment for sin, retreats before the Son. It would perhaps be possible for it to retreat in such a way that its boundaries would merely be pushed back; man could, for example, reach an older age of life. Lazarus, however, is already three days dead. Here, it is death itself that obeys the Lord's word. A human voice reaches where none has ever sounded before. Something becomes reversible that had always been irreversible. The dead are subject to the Father's creative power, and here the Son of Man receives power over this reserved area. He receives it from the Father's love because of his obedience, so that by this miracle he might shed light on his relationship to the Father anew. By his obedience, which knows no boundaries, he shows the likewise unlimited power of God.

At the healing of the woman with the hemorrhage, "a power goes out from him": the miracle weakens him because in this obedience of the miracle the obedience of the Cross is already implied in advance, and divine-human obedience always means a challenge to mere nature. But he always works the miracle because he sees in the vision of the Father that the Father desires it. In every miracle, he does the Father's will and not his own.

✸ ✸ ✸

On the Cross he will suffer as a mere man. While working miracles, the God-man makes use of a power that dwells within him—he *can* work miracles—but it is a power he administers entirely in obedience. Each time it is as though he placed everything back in the hands of the Father so that the Father himself might give the Spirit of the miracle and therein reveal anew his bond with the Son. This bond he reveals, not to strengthen the Son, but so that the Son can give Christian truth new clarity.

Obedience unto death can be traced through the Lord's entire life; but it probably becomes clearest where the Lord accomplishes the unexpected, breaching the laws that the Father has laid upon men in order to display the fatherly power anew. This breaching also reveals that the Son, who is himself God and perfect, is not necessarily himself subject to these laws that have been laid upon sinners. He does not obey any worldly power, but God alone. But he does so with a tremendous obedience from which every Christian obedience derives and which is so strong that across the millennia it has lost none of its power.

And if the Lord allows his saints to work miracles, these are always miracles that test especially their obedience, which for a moment lend to their obedience his own visage. The Lord lets his saints become conspicuous with his own conspicuousness. For the miracles that a saint works do not belong to him. They are imposed upon him by God himself as a burden of obedience. The saint must perform them in order to show that he is ready to co-carry out that obedience which the Lord lived before him and to do so to the extent that is pleasing to the Lord. He must show that he is ready, too, to step outside everyday obedience for a moment and welcome this striking obedience. If Paul says: "I no longer live, but Christ lives in me", he knows about the Lord's miracles. He knows that the obedience he owes the Lord could extend so far that there would even be space therein for miracles. And he may not think for a moment that he performs them by his own strength or by the excellence of his obedience.

Miracles always reveal something of the living presence of eternal life. They break through the passing Today in order to let in the eternal Today. The final passing Today is death. So the Son, who dies on the Cross, prepares the miracle of his Resurrection in death. He reveals that he obeys the Father to such an extent that within the scope of his mission he fulfills even the task of dying on the Cross. Every act of obedience is a fulfillment. With men, it is a fulfillment of faith; with God, it is a fulfillment of love. But God gives to his own, who are obedient out of faith, love—or what amounts to the same thing, he pours into them in their obedience of faith something of the Son's eternal obedience of love. By this infused obedience, he suspends boundaries, measurement, and insight, so that miracles become possible—whether God requires them of his saint now or not. In the Son's obedience of the Cross, all boundaries are negated: so by obedience unto death, the eternal life of the Resurrection can crack the absolute limit: death.

Obedience unto Death

By letting the Hour be veiled and leaving it entirely to the Father's discretion, the Son hands over to him the whole course of the work of the Passion, which arrives without fail. But when it does come, all at once it brings time to an end. The normal course of time is annulled. At the outset of the Passion, the Son is wrapped in a night that as such is experienced as timeless. It simply *is*; it does not run. The Son's attitude in this night is that of not attempting to escape from it. He does not put it off until later; he does not experience it as something that comes and goes; he remains in it and accomplishes what the

Father expects of him. He has handed the Hour over to him, so it is removed from the course of time. As long as the suffering lasts, he suffers in the everpresent moment, without having any hope for an end or a gauge of its length and without his dying making any progress. That is part of the obedience of this Hour. Outwardly, he will die like any mortal. Interiorly, however, he is laden with the anguish of humanity. Every single sin that he bears rounds up to the entire agony, which surpasses the measure of his ability to endure. From beginning to end, he is simply overwhelmed. No suffering after him will ever be comparable to his, because everything was in it. So much so that nothing can be pried out of it or brought into comparison with it. Only after his death can time resume its normal course once more. Until then—even if men know about time—it remains for the Son utterly broken. He must endure in the indivisibility of an immeasurable period, so that every sin really fills him up, and, for the one suffering, nothing else is visible anymore but night and the God-forsakenness of sin.

This is the fullness of obedience: that he takes everything into himself just as the Father intends it and can alone intend it, while no person will ever appreciate what really happened there. In order to fulfill the will of the Father, the Son constantly *sought* it. This search was a perfect opening, so perfect that it exhausts absolutely everything that is—even all sin

and distance from God—so that all may be fulfilled.
Dying, the Son of Man, in his obedient, world-
encompassing seeking, encounters the Creator of the
world, to whom all order is subject. It is the most
supreme order, that this encounter occurs through
obedience. For the Son, nothing more remains of
his own will, his own discretion, his own foresight
and judgment about what is right; he has transferred
everything to the Father in obedience. It is the obedience of total love, which alone is capable of bearing
everything unto death, indeed, beyond death—and
this "beyond" will be the descent into hell.

Even death itself and the going-down is pure
obedience, which nothing can surpass. As the Lord's
birth reveals the Father's will to found obedience for
the world anew, so the Lord's death reveals that the
fullness of this foundation has been accomplished.
Now the time has come. And so discipleship appears
in the New Testament to begin here on the Cross.
The whole life of the Son, in which he is revealed
to us, is a succession of ever new ways in which the
New Covenant gives strength and confirmation.
But the ultimate power that will allow even normal
people to imitate the Son and a genuine apostolate
to belong to the New Covenant—this power is only
set free with his death, because here is accomplished
the highest obedience, beyond which there can be
nothing more. For here everything is dissolved into
this obedience of the Son's love for the Father.

Jesus' words on the Cross—those that sound as though they were spoken to himself, those directed to the Father, those to the Mother and to the Beloved Disciple—are pure beginnings. They are new foundations of obedience for men. It is as though now heaven and earth, tormentor and beloved, and he himself and his Spirit united in order to let obedience come forth anew. Everything attainable is brought together in order to be inseparably interwoven. The knot itself, though, is the Son's obedience.

The Resurrection and the Ascension as Obedience

The Lord expressed for a moment the wish that the chalice might pass from him. But then he drank it to its depths. He drank it so completely that he died from it and in death experienced nothing more than the severity and inexorability of obedience. Then the Resurrection arrives, which is no less a work of obedience. The Father awakens the Son to life, and now there is as little resistance in the Son as there was earlier. Resurrection is pure letting be.

Magdalen does not recognize him at the grave. The most extreme obedience of the Cross and of hell has transformed him. It is not only death and the women's judgment that he had died which now render him unrecognizable, but the perfection of

his absolute obedience by which he has been transformed into what the Father willed. Only faith,
which is newly bestowed upon the women, can
take away the unfamiliarity and impart to obedience
a direction and a sense that can recognize the One
who has reached obedience's end. This recognition
is of great importance both for him and for everyone who gets to see him in obedience, because the
Lord *must* lay new standards upon his followers; he
cannot content himself any longer with what people are inclined to bestow of their own accord, but
must constantly apply to the faithful the measurement he has realized—however mercifully.

The Lord must impart to the Church something
of what he has accomplished so that her imitation
can be authentic: not only something from the obedience of the Cross, but also from the obedience
of the Resurrection. Were there no obedience of
the Resurrection, the Church's obedience would
be sucked down into darkness, into sadness, into the
pain of death. Ecclesial obedience, however, should
be one that is full of confidence, for each and every
person who lives in faith, whether he seeks to carry
it out himself, or whether at least he sees it carried
out by others, for example, by the saints. In this
way, death and resurrection are like two phases of
the obedience of discipleship.

The Resurrection is also of great significance for
the disciples, who get to know the Lord afresh in the

new dimension of the Forty Days. These days are an abiding appeal to faith and obedience. When the Lord still lived with them as one among them and his suffering, death, and Resurrection were still to come, his mysteries appeared to them more clearly. Sure, they understood little, but this little was to them more lucid, and with it they could, within the metrics of their daily life, somehow initiate something. Now everything is veiled in the exceedingly great mystery. Their faith is not only fulfilled, but over-fulfilled, and they are overwhelmed in the way of the mystery. And yet the Lord's command to follow only now attains its full urgency. There is nothing more between them and him: no deferring, no avoiding. They are placed on the way of obedience that leads through the Lord to the Father: a way of radically letting-be and yet also of action and of self-determination.

From now on, obedience has attained far richer aspects for the disciples, and its vitality gives way to the divine. The obedience that the Lord has accomplished draws the obedient ones after him and leads them, too, where they do not wish to go. They are now ones who are led, and their being led lies among the mysteries of the Lord's death and Resurrection. A meeting continuously takes place of death and life, world and heaven, transience and eternity. Moreover, faith, love, and hope should receive new power daily in order to be used the way the Lord constantly uses the mystery of his obedience: to bring us in this way closer to the essence of the Triune God. All fields of faith, and of human life in faith, are touched and formed anew by this obedience.

And if, then, the Ascension arrives and the Son in this moment reveals only the single movement upward to the Father, this is like one last arrow of his obedience that does not slip away in order to be free, does not separate itself in order to take its own course, but rather leads everything—even his own mission and himself, the one sent—back to the sending Father in such a straight-line of obedience that he chooses the shortest path. Thus, at the Ascension one can see anew the greatness of the Son's obedience: it is the unification of the Son with the Father in the Holy Spirit. This union is accomplished by the accomplished mission, by taking along everyone whom the Son came to save and whom he saved not so much by his presence and the testimonies of love shown to them as by his obedience. His obedience pervaded every hidden day, every smallest action as much as everything great that we know of the Lord. The unity of his existence absolutely lies in his obedience. And because we, too, may become obedient in his discipleship, this whole existence acquires the meaning of a model and a source of strength within the space of the Church, which the Son founded by pure obedience to the Father.

4

Obedience in Heaven

Obedience as Participation in God

Man can attempt to obey God in order to come to know him—in order to attain, by the strengthening of his faith that has been granted him, a deeper experience of divine love. He can thus connect with obedience a goal that is supposed to bring him nearer to God in the Spirit. He keeps the commandments, loves his neighbor, always thinking about God in order to experience his divine will in itself. But the reverse can also happen: that a person so loves God, so worships him, that he becomes obedient from a knowledge of the faith. He hollows himself out in order to let God have the whole space within himself. Both kinds of obedience have, of course, their ultimate meaning in God himself, and God himself can show man these two ways of obedience in order to bind man to himself and to teach him to love better.

But once man stands in eternal life before God, such a love and such a power to worship will be given to him by God that obedience will follow as though of itself. Every consideration of whether he should obey God falls away; obedience is a form of love's fulfillment, of existence itself, before and in God. Everything that makes obedience more difficult on earth: one's own self that desires something other, the question of whether it suits me or not, sin—all of this disappears in heaven. Man brings forth from himself obedience as a tree brings forth a ripe fruit: the fruit of the redemption by the Son, the fruit of being created by the Father for the Son. Obedience ennobles existence in heaven and gives it at every eternal moment its ultimate meaning. Obedience fulfills man's love still more than it did on earth and gives him the power to worship in truth. Obedience in heaven is at the same time the result of the final purification; man is so purified that he can only love and obey—both have completely lost the character of a duty; all they have left is the spirit of eternal gratitude for the squandering of the Son of God for men.

The infinite multitude that is seen in heaven bears the features of obedience without exception. And because these are at the same time also the features of love, man sees the Triune Love radiating everywhere in heaven: in its exchange, but also in the way that everything is *integrated* into it. God

lives for God; but he invited man to enter into his
Triune exchange. He does not conceal his mystery
of love behind mysterious walls; he reveals himself.
And this self-disclosure suffices to transfer the beatitude of eternal life into man, and this beatitude is
in them the wish and will to obey in everything the
law of the divine exchange. Joy and obedience are
simply one, and they are love.

And if man pursues events on earth from heaven,
he grasps the intentions of God from his new obedience. He has been swayed to God's side; sin no
longer has for him anything tempting. He can,
included in the mystery of sinlessness, hardly still
explain how men on earth get themselves into con-
fusion, infatuation, and powerlessness, into bonds
that hinder them from being obedient.

He looks to God in everything. And from God
he can love what he otherwise could not love
because it appears to him unintelligible and inaccessible. He learns to love the enigmatic in the light
of the love of God and hardly notices how far from
all the tedious considerations and decisions of the
world the final purification has brought him; he
lives where obedience, love, and joy are an insepa-
rable unity.

That the Father gives men this gift of unity
through the suffering of the Son is not only promised in the Church, but is already foreshadowed in
some ecclesial events: for example, in the fact that

the one who receives Communion receives something of the Son's obedience, a beginning that he
knows well is unfolded to a fullness in heaven—or
in the fact that the one who confesses has been set
free by absolution from the bonds of sin, and at his
prayer of thanks the joyful notion shakes him that
this is a foretaste of heavenly existence toward whose
great obedience he plans to move with little earthly
steps. Everywhere in the Church, pillars rise that
appear built up toward a heavenly vault, indeed, are
actually designed by it, since the Church strives to
make every grace of obedience, which God gives
to the world through the existence of the Son, usable
for the life of men. The Church administers what
in heaven no longer requires administration because
here it has become natural. From afar she points
toward the fullness that is promised the one who
believes, to which he first approaches in hope that
the bonds that still hold him here shall one day fall.

Obedience as Marian Love

Whoever does not love cannot obey in a Christian
manner. Christian obedience necessarily includes
love. Out of love for God, and also out of love for
the life God gave her, Mary gave the angel her assent
and thereby proclaimed that she willed to take up
her mission, that out of love she *also* gives her assent
to this mission. This encounter of Mary with the

angel is the pure essence of obedience; it is a con-
centration of her love for God and of her life in a
single point, and this point means: the acceptance of
the mission. Whoever obeys always takes his mission anew upon himself. On earth this is connected
to all the difficulties of human life; in heaven, however, the assent unfolds in a sphere beyond every
difficulty. Thus, Mary lives in heaven in continuity
with her earthly obedience, which was able to be
carried on without interruption into eternal life so
that the single point spreads out to eternity. In this
expansion, her life is so bountiful that every obedience of the world in the Son's discipleship finds
itself there as in its core. She is the one who mediates ever anew the grace of the Yes to the task; with
her, it immediately becomes clear that obedience
is constantly an acceptance in love. The connection of every Christian obedience with the obedience of the Mother can be traced visibly (more or
less clearly) in the life of the Christian; it is indeed
hidden in faith, but it can be still more certainly
ascertained because every grace of the obedience
of Christians branches off from the grace of Mary's
single assent, and there they all gather again. Earthly
obedience attains through her also a fullness in
heaven, which it would not have from itself alone.
She receives what rises up in requests, commenda-
tions, and thanksgivings in order to communicate
this to the Son and through the Son to the Father.

In this interplay of grace, in which the gravity of being sent and the security of earthly missions are simultaneously manifested in the eternal, the Mother also shows how faithful she remains to her initial commitment. "Let it be done unto me according to your word": and the Word was done in her and remained eternally alive so that it now has its place in heaven. The fulfillment of Mary's life, which was already possible on earth because of the purity of Mary's love, now radiates a power in heaven in which all receive a share without thereby detracting from the Mother's portion. Precisely now, when most live from her, she herself lives most securely in unconditional obedience. She lives in an unchanging obedience that means everything to her because it is accepted by God and by all of heaven.

Obedience without Bounds

The obedience that the Son suffers on earth unto his death has meaning for him not only because the Father demands it, but also because he can pass it on to others. He takes from people their resistance and establishes an immediate relationship between himself and the sinner. He has the power to sow obedience in sinners, to deepen what incipient obedience is at hand and expand it beyond its boundaries; he can make the obedience, within the one obeying, into a marvel for the natural world. In heaven, obedience is not at all restricted by any limitation of sin and contradiction. There, it is an act of boundlessness placed in the heart of eternal life and taking part in the action of the infinite.

Even in heaven Mary obeys, not for herself, but for humanity, in order to clear for it the path to the Son. The graces she thus mediates are always likewise the graces of her obedience. On earth, men remain, even in the Church, caught within their limits; they bump up against their own sins and those of others. They feel how their obedience shatters against invisible walls, how they do not hold to what they have promised and how they are incapable of perfect fidelity. This is where Mary can enter: even in heaven her assent is available to those on earth. She takes the barriers and boundaries away from those who are inhibited and confined, and she fulfills in heaven what we on earth would like to do but cannot and gives us the result in its proper form. Her heavenly form bears fruit within the world.

Mary is not the only one in heaven who obeys perfectly, however. They all obey and the fruitfulness of each mixes with the fruitfulness of the obedience of all. The saints and the angels who live in the Trinitarian exchange of love enable the Church to participate in the fruits of their obedience, which they, for their part, distribute among believers. This participation cannot be measured as something finite because it derives from heaven; it is at most restricted by the limited capacity of the imperfect on earth. Such an earthly person knows that he receives infinitely more than he gives; he knows also that it is a matter of the Christian grace of obedience— that even where he senses his limitations, something boundless lives within him. This is the promise for him. He, the sinful, inhibited one, will not remain forever bound within his restraints. Indeed, he can now already act beyond them because his obedience meets a heavenly, perfect obedience.

The obedience of the saints in heaven is not without relation to their earthly tasks. Something personal, singular, and distinctive has remained for each of them. The zeal of obedience, the place of preference that a saint takes through his particular action retains its distinctive character. An Ignatius is also in heaven himself, just as a little Thérèse remains faithful because God himself gives her this fidelity, has formed her character, and has achieved something from her humility, which he needs and which is essential for the Church. Thus the obedience of each saint unfolds according to his personality but also under the immediate influence of the obedience of Mary and ultimately within the ambit of the obedience of Christ to the Father; from now on, the saint's obedience is freed and expanded, for even the saints had their limitations on earth. Only in heaven do they grasp the full boundlessness of obedience. To be sure, the saint was already obeying on earth, ready to perform more than he naturally could; yet, precisely by the urge within him for the More, he came up against his limitations even where he overcame them, whereas now in heaven he has come to enjoy boundless obedience. This belongs to his holiness, to his eternal joy. And if he intercedes, whether by his own initiative or because he has been called upon, he places his own boundlessness at the world's disposal, and here and there something develops that corresponds to his intention and character, even if here below it does not attain its complete unfolding. For there is no human work— not even if it is unfolded entirely within the will of God—that could be perfected on earth. But, nevertheless, there is continually an exchange between heaven and earth, an augmentation of life on earth on the basis of obedience in heaven, but also an augmentation of the resistance in heaven against sin, which continues to exist on earth.

And there are also the angels in heaven who obey like children who have the opportunity to show how they love, how well-behaved they are, and how they fit themselves into whatever is going on. If one can still descry in Mary's obedience to the Father the traces of her earthly obedience and, where she prevails, sense the overcoming of difficulty, this is not the case with the angels. Their obedience appears as though supernatural; one angel is not even placed more in the service of absolute obedience than another. Obedience seems like an aspect of their game, like a way of their being. One cannot separate their manner of inserting themselves from how one thinks of them. One cannot discover any more or less in this or draw any comparison. So much does obedience belong to their essence that it hardly needs to be emphasized. It is simply there, intrinsically and uniformly, characteristic of the whole collective of the angels, but not singly, as one attribute that could be named among others.

5

Untinged Obedience

The Absolute Point

In his petition, "Not my will, but yours be done", the Son grants us a glimpse into his obedience. He possesses a will of his own; the drinking of the cup—one could say—does not suit this will. But he transcends this will and gives preference to the Father's will. This he does out of love, the same love in which he undertook his mission and carried it out up to this point and in which he will suffer and surrender his spirit into the hands of the Father.—If we consider Mary's obedience during the years the Son was with her, therein we see her love clearly: she loves her son, and she loves, too, the mission the Son has brought her, and out of this love she is obedient.—If a person decides upon the life of the counsels, love lies at the base of his resolution: out of love for God and for the call he has heard from God, he will acquiesce to the obedience of the religious order.

Considering the life of the Lord, it is not difficult to sense in every action and in every prayer his love as the fundamental motive of his existence: love for the Father and for obeying him, for the apostles, for all people whom he addresses and for whom he works miracles, for the poor whom he meets, for the sinners whose guilt he takes onto the Cross. No less does one find the motive of love everywhere in Mary's life. Likewise with a member of a religious order an underground love must be present, even if it remains covered, perhaps momentarily or for a longer time; even where his obedience is deficient, he stands under the sign of the original love of his life-choice. Because, however, each person possesses a personality, he imparts to his actions, even those of the deepest obedience, a personal imprint. One does not demand of him that he obey like a machine or create out of an anonymous store of love in the Church in order to carry out the action of one who remains anonymous, that he foster the trains of thought and speak the prayers of one who remains anonymous. He remains the personality God created and willed him to be.

From the rules of the great orders there comes to us something that corresponds to the spirit, will, and obedience of the founder. He desires to do everything for God and really attempts to do so; self-denial is not understood by him and demanded in such a way that he would have to smear the grace corresponding to his personal task into anonymity. It is part of his gratitude to God that he makes himself known as the one whom God intended, not out of vanity or ambition, but simply out of obedience, because he—Ignatius or Benedict—received the task of laboring with the talent he obtained. Thus, these founders demand from their people obedience on the grounds of the life of the Lord, but also on the grounds of the order's rule. They demand obedience, not in a tension between the Lord and the founders of the order (or his followers and representatives), but rather in a certain polar supplement: this is the will of the Lord, this is the will of the founder that gives God the glory and desires to serve him perfectly. But the way he worships God and desires service remains characteristic for him. If a religious lives earnestly *within* his rule and attempts to follow it as attentively as possible, then it can be that he becomes for his fellow men an image of the rule, an image of Christ through the rule, an image of God through the rule and submission to Christ. He would thus stand in a certain filiation, although it would not be easy actually to prove it objectively and historically at each step. Perhaps one would have to return to the Old Testament: to the sacrifice of Abraham, then to the sacrifice on the Cross, to the sacrifice of the founder of the order, and from there to the sacrifice required by the founder, as the rule provides for it. And at the end would stand the individual religious, who with his obedience gives his personal imprint to religious obedience. This must be so, because he is an individual who stands free before God and possesses his own will. He has professed the vows and has thereby marked his freedom anew, shaping his freedom once again by this present decision.

❋ ❋ ❋

In the core of obedience, however, there is a point that consists only of a Yes and No. I do it, or I do not do it. I assent, or I refuse. This is so raw, so rough, unrefined that this point alone decides: acceptance or rejection. Everything else—motives, the character of the order, or personal expression— all of this is completely irrelevant here and has disappeared. One finds himself at a source, at *untinged* obedience. Here lies the assent of the Mother, the assent of the Son to his mission, perfectly evident, beyond all discussion and everything right. The Son and the Mother have never argued, but followers sometimes do, precisely because they want to follow the rule, to lean on the Son and Mother for support, and to carry out in some fashion the sacrifice of Abraham.

Once the reflection and arguing begin, the one who obeys enters into the zone of *tinged* obedience. In the original Yes, however, it was evident one needed to act without qualification and nuance because the voice one hears, the act one undertakes, the reply one gives—these come from what is absolutely original. They posit something that unfolds in the depth of the soul before God, that proclaims a belonging to him without color or hue, without glitter, without focusing on others' possible imitations or on the fact that others have already carried out something similar. What occurs is not far from the obedience of Adam before the fall into sin; it is close to God's question to Adam, from whom only obedience and not-sinning are expected. God receives such obedience in Christ. But from the grace of Christ he gives to each person in the presence of his Son and Spirit the possibility of saying a Yes of complete discipleship, the possibility of placing in one's innermost core an event of obedience farther within than any possible "no" or "maybe" or "later". Where the beginning is. The source.

Here, the person is permitted to be a creator by allowing to come into being what God expects of him and what will thus be the meaning of his whole existence. He can only do it *without witnesses*, in solitude, and yet under the force of having been requested, which completely dictates to him his response as though he were robbed at that moment of every freedom—and this, because freedom is so great that it exceeds him, and he can no longer see it but only from the focal point of its flame cry out his response.

The Effect

The first effect of this kind of obedience is reflected
in one's own life by the fact that every thought about
one's own performance, one's own path, one's own
significance completely withdraws. The one who
obeys is pure dedication. God alone can demand and
effect such obedience. And the one obeying can in
the moment that the act is committed so withdraw
that he does not need to give an account of his deed,
in a sense, neither before God nor before himself.
He is upheld; he does what is right; his decision is
valid. It is not as though he acted in the moment like
a sleepwalker, but he is somewhat like the visionary
who glimpses something of the world beyond, who
is *beside himself*, because what he has experienced lies
beyond whatever could be grasped. This being beside
oneself enjoys a protection that can only come from
God, even though it remains veiled and invisible.

Later, once the state of the untinged obedience
has passed, one must learn anew to take the steps
toward his task. If he stands, for example, under
the weight of a rule, under the eye of a superior
upon a path of life that is, as far as necessary, clearly
predestined for him, he will recall the state of the
untinged obedience as though it were a *miracle*. He
will not comprehend it and yet will ascertain that
everything decisive happened there, that his present efforts—and even his joy—to be permitted to

obey, had in that moment their origin. From that point, the power still flows to him, God's power, and he can only visualize it as such if he looks back along the path to the origin that has never been lost—if the present moment stands in a clear connection with that past moment. By the power of his present obedience, he can do things, or allow them to happen, that directly connect him to what he decided upon in that moment, his joy, namely, to rest himself unprotected in God's hands and to correspond solely to the will of God. What he completes today is only the visible result of that invisible event; this latter event has its remote effects, since the later decisions originate from what was earlier incomplete; the late certainty originates from an original unknowing. In the rational life (for even in faith there lies a *ratio*), the non-rational, that is, what had not become clear, lay wrapped within an act of obedience, which in one moment had an impact forever and remains unrepeatable. Once I was so beyond myself that what happened to me determined me for all the future.[1]

---

[1] It can happen that for some individuals the power of the assent to the life of the counsels appears to be exhausted with the initial act of assent; afterward, they only limp along. Yet the initial power should remain lively enough in all that follows.

6

Christian Obedience

Integration into Christ

God's Son becomes man in obedience, and his whole
human life remains the expression of his initial obedience. On the one hand, it is an obedience we can
understand, insofar as the Lord continually places
landmarks by which we can orient ourselves because
they are, at least sometimes, legible for us. On the
other hand, this obedience is embedded within a
mystery between the Son and the Father, and this
mystery accompanies everything human and visible
under a veil. We know about its existence; there are
also moments when the Lord speaks with us about
it, and we inhale something of it. Most of it, however, unfolds for us in secret.

And now since as believers we should walk a path
of discipleship, we must take the Lord's obedience
for the example of our discipleship *just as it is*, open
and veiled, comprehensible and incomprehensible.
It certainly cannot be a matter of reproducing the

events of the life of the Lord; it cannot be a matter of rendering the situations of his time merely past occurances or simulations and of making rough-and-ready reproductions in our own environment from which we form the decisions of our obedience. Our obedience, therefore, must proceed from the everyday life that has already been established for us and that we have already discovered. Indeed, I can—in the style of Ignatian contemplation—think myself together with my environment back into the time of the Lord; the bedroom in which I reside, I can compare with the space where the Lord stayed, and so forth, in order to call the Spirit of Christ's obedience more vividly into my life. I can set the work he did in relation to mine in order better to adopt the Spirit of his work: but at the most I can do this as a *preparation* for my concrete act of obedience, as something that, indeed, can render good services in the period of observation, but that can nevertheless abandon me in the moment of "now or never". Perhaps I thought my way too much into a fictitious environment; the circumstances are different, or my reflection remained stuck at the theoretical level, and right now it cannot capture my current situation.

Thus, even if we evoke so many images from the life of the Lord, it is inevitably necessary to live according to his Spirit in our daily life and to reflect him in as undiminished a way as possible. This can be the fruit of the grace of countless contemplations; it can, however, also be the fruit of the grace of a plain readiness to hear the voice of the Lord everywhere. For, there is the one path: to arrange the situation in which we are today or in which we could be tomorrow or at some point. There is, however, the other path of letting this situation go and of remaining alone in prayer, in the presence of Christ and his constantly offered grace, trusting that the intercession of the Church and of all the saints—all of whom were and still are in a situation of obedience—will obtain for us the grace of obedience; on this latter path, one does this, not because of a calculation, but from a plain, *universal* readiness for obedience, in which we are permitted to remain. This universality does not threaten the particular, for from the perspective of this universal, we can constantly assess the particular. Moreover, we know the situations in which we failed and can determine the extent of the failure—not in a brooding way, but quickly and succinctly—in order to be free by this general readiness once more for new particular situations in which we want to do it better. Thus, in the sacrament of penance, the confession is also only a beginning so that the important thing can then follow, and the grace of God's forgiveness can pour out over the penitent. We can, however, also look back to the Lord from our situation and ask ourselves how he, in our position, would have carried out the obedience, with a view to *his* universal readiness to fulfill the will of the Father completely even before the particular situation became apparent to him.

Still beyond this lies the many things in the Lord's obedience that play out in the silence of the mystery between him and the Father. Even if we can never comprehend this, we know that it is a mystery of the obedience of love. This ineffable aspect is the Son's focus and the source of everything that becomes visible of him; it becomes visible, not as an approximation, but as a precise correspondence to what remains hidden. We who are supposed to follow the Lord must therefore attempt, in the silence of prayer and adoration into which the Lord himself directs us, to ask the Father to integrate our presence into that of his Son, our being-here into his being-everywhere, our weak readiness into his strong readiness, our presently demanded Christian obedience into his perpetually theanthropic obedience, so that by faith we partake of his ineffable mystery of obedience. May God form our discipleship according to his goodwill and according to the decree he set over us. May God form our Yes into an emulation of the perfect Yes of his Son.

For such an integration to become possible, a simplification of all of our relationships must follow. We are then, in prayer before God, no longer *these* particular subjects who speak from out of *this* particular situation in order to experience how they can serve God today or tomorrow. Everything scattered is veiled for a time, and we plead to God in deep ignorance. We are any sinner before the merciful God, and this sinner begs to be received and for the favor of being able to follow obediently. In the moment, he does not need his imaginative powers to envision his particular situation. He thanks God that he has been allowed the place of solitude and may plead here very modestly: to plead, not that my will be done, but yours, without pitting the two wills against each other or defining them against each other and without suggesting any possible exchanges between the two. God's will should be for me so great that my will is only like a whisper, indeed, is actually only mentioned in order to remind the Father that the Son, too, prayed with these words and to ask him to assign a place for our obedience within that of the Son. It does not matter where we are now, how great our achievement is, how much we can promise, indeed, what we are willing to keep. All of this should remain hidden, so long as it pleases God; if he displays something of it, this is good; but if he displays nothing, this should be no less acceptable to us.

The Negative and Anxiety

God can reveal by *constructing* something positive: a house, a path, a direction. This house, this path, and this direction are things that the one praying somehow perceives: they fall within his realm; he knows he is designated for them. God can, however, also reveal by *omitting*. He can give such a sharp outline to the borders, to that which is not possible or not desirable, that the center that remains undetermined becomes clear and the one praying knows that he has to arrange something there. God indicates to him this empty space, and only his obedience can fill it out. He cannot do this by himself, but with the grace of God, who also prepared the space. It is more difficult for the one who obeys to fill out an omission because it can become easily confused with one's own intentions, with the rounding out of something one thought up oneself, so that the obedience initially planned suddenly turns into the execution of one's own will. Thus, the Christian must always pray afresh, ask, sense, enter the omitted space—which can seem to be as empty as night—must insert himself into it and be conformed to its shape, always asking God whether it is right thus.

If God shows positively, the believer certainly must also pray that he will behave as God desires, pray so that he will not make it too easy for himself or erect his own buildings in the place where God began to build. But prayer into the void is another, more difficult thing, because it can belong to God's plan that the one praying—even if he is in the right spot—should be completely enshrouded by darkness and not intuit what is correct. In this case, one must inquire relentlessly; the shout can become a cry for help from out of anxiety, into anxiety. For anxiety does not dwell in positive buildings; it lives where there is a void, which at times is specially hollowed out for it. This anxiety can then penetrate into that prayer, can echo through it and drown out everything else so that, in comparison, nothing else is found to make a sound anymore. And because of this anxiety, nothing else is perceptible anymore.

This anxiety, then, is the strictest obedience of a John of the Cross; it is also the obedience of the Disciple on Patmos who undergoes the terrifying scenes of the apocalypse. It is like a supernothing within nothing, like a second hollowing out of non-being. It is like a second recess within recess itself, which appears to negate the first recess, erasing the limits that give it meaning, apparently dissolving everything meaningful up to this point, because God also needs this form of obedience. It is no longer the obedience of the Mount of Olives but actually the obedience of the Cross. And it is also not the anxiety of the Mount of Olives, but the anxiety of the Lord on the Cross, who not only spends himself unto death, but to the same end spends also his anxiety. And the Lord cannot bury it in his unique death, but rather, because it belongs to the Father and the Father gives it to him, he too wants to confer it upon those who are his so that they may draw nearer to him in obedience and so that the Father may better know him in them. It can be a dreadful anxiety in which contours are still visible. Yet even this dread can ultimately dissolve itself into something completely formless and become the dark of impenetrable night whose black, however, can also suddenly, in ultimate hopelessness, turn into the red of the burning pool. It is not easy to imagine that obedience can be carried out through all of these levels, that some, from the moment they promised obedience to God, go through life without questioning, fulfilling their mission, being led from one task to another, and that, for them, every cause for doubt has ceased. Meanwhile, others, who at first seemed just as calm and knew their way, were pushed by obedience into the most terrible adventure of faith in order to arrive at the very place they desired to avoid at any cost, where every view is blocked. Still, each is a response to God: a response to the desire for discipleship that the Son cherishes, a response to the Father's need to join brothers to his Son and, at the same time, a response to the cry of all humanity for redemption.

Hell and Resurrection

As a true steward, the Son finally hands over his Spirit to the Father on the Cross and thereby carries out the last thing he had to accomplish. It is an act of complete interior loneliness. He goes into death without his Spirit. It is, however, no arbitrary action, for he must bear loneliness and abandonment until the end. It is obedience, which merely does what is proper to obedience, without caring in the least for the consequences, without asking what will come from it. Perhaps, if he had kept his Spirit for himself, this would have brought him some relief or given him certain insights in death. But everything alleviating and illuminating must now yield so that there can be absolute night. There is no longer the least space for anything other than the obedience of death. A few saints were granted to undergo something similar, not by their own power, but by the Lord's power, which accompanied them so much that they could bear the abandonment that shadowed over them so much and were permitted to experience this ultimate obedience. Protectively, the Lord takes them into his own night.

The Son did not rise from the Cross but, rather, after his death experienced the descent into hell. From there the Father awakened him, the Father who gives the night and also the light, who already at the creation of the world separated the night from the day and bestowed upon both their particular meanings. Was the separation of day and night at that time already a parable for the man who was most abandoned in obedience and who would be led over into the most unifying light? In any case, the transition is for man the expression of purest obedience. Man cannot be more obedient than by giving even his innermost disposition into the hands of the Father so that he can tune it to be joyful or sorrowful. In prayer, the believer knows that the Father will dispose of both. But when he is in the night, he no longer knows this, in order to experience the mood of the night completely. If he plunges back into joy, this also will not be marred by the memory of the night he suffered or by the apprehension of what is to come. As previously he was enabled to suffer perfectly, so now he is set free to rejoice perfectly: free to live in God anew, in the discipleship of the risen Lord.

But even this freedom is obedience. If the Christian were no longer completely obedient, he would also enjoy merely a restricted freedom. He would see the boundaries everywhere, sense everywhere yesterday and tomorrow; he would no longer be completely available for the God-given moment; he would no longer have the fullness of prayer that God had offered to him and could no longer experience the fullness of the presence of God. Everything would be subordinate to his consideration and assessment, and thus would his experience be restricted. Obedience, however: as earlier he saw the desolation and hopelessness of his position, so he is now permitted to share the complete Christian joy that is itself participation in the Resurrection of the Lord.

If the Lord in the joyful season of the Forty Days must occasionally speak words of reproach and admonition and must touch upon things that are not only life and joy, he does this out of the same indifference of that obedience of his in which he died and rose. It belongs to his mission. He must proclaim, interpret, and confirm these things, must relate everything past and everything coming in its reality, and must give everything in the world its meaning. In these words of the Resurrection, he fulfills his command to love one's neighbor. His admonitions are love; they show to those whom he has redeemed new paths that lead through him to the Father. By just being redeemed, not everything is accomplished. He must bind those who are his own to new responsibilities precisely because they are redeemed and because they were able to see vividly on the Cross what threatened them; it is now interpreted for them by the Risen One. Their understanding means new joys for them that derive from the joy of the Lord. By now being able to believe in their Redeemer, they are prepared even to walk in *his* paths, not by their own power and caprice, but rather in an obedience that wells up from his obedience.

7

Obedience in the World

Family

The various social structures in which a human life is embedded require the integration of each person in a manner not far removed from true obedience. In the family, the child must obey the parents, and the woman must be subject to her husband, but the man must accept responsibility for the family. An order thus forms with which each member of the family, as long as it persists, must reckon. One's work, whether in the factory or in the office, will not proceed successfully without strict obedience: times are defined, the kind of work, the responsibility to the employer, to the material, to the work to be realized, to one's co-workers: everything constrains the freedom of the laborer. There are processes of work where all the laborers must interlock like cogs in a machine. Those who participate therein can usually measure the correctness of the measures in view of the quality of the product and the pace of production. Admittedly, everything ultimately comes down to numbers, to deadlines that must be met, and production quotas. What is human about the worker, his disposition, his wishes, these play a slight, presumably ever smaller role. Perhaps someone was trained for a job that can only be performed in a certain context, and he loses his position and falls into a predicament because his advanced age and his social relationships do not allow for any further change. Perhaps there remains as the only solution work that does not at all suit him, but he must defer; resignation has already become for him second nature; to want to grasp why it must be so is just as useless for him as a rebellion against destiny. Some worker who has toiled during the day at the most cramped post would like, when he returns home in the evening, to have the roles reversed: not only to be free, but to be the master, to be able to impose his will on others. The woman and the children are supposed to obey; the neighbors are supposed to conform themselves to him. In some circumstances, it takes a lot for him to see that an abuse of his obedience at work does not enable him to abuse the obedience of his companions, to see that it is rather up to him to promote the order of obedience in his circle of relations by using his responsibility properly.

The person who has only predefined work to accomplish will have the urge to invent something. This drive belongs not only to the nature of the person; it belongs to the nature of obedience, and not only to worldly obedience, but even to ecclesial obedience and to the obedience of religious life. The one who obeys is never a dead instrument but is, rather, a living spirit. And the obedience is never a mechanical principle but is, rather, an organic one; in the Church, it is even a principle of divine liveliness: Jesus Christ himself. In the parable of the Gospel, the faithful servants exert in obedience their spirit and their inventive powers in order to increase the talents of their Lord; and his praise shows that he wanted their service to be understood in just this way.

For the father of the family, inventing and creating is also the production of an organic order of obedience within the family. Some things about this order are predetermined: while he is at work, his wife takes care of the housework and cares for the children; her daytime can be more strictly divided than that of her husband. Other things remain to be determined: the children understand obedience poorly; at school and on the street, they come into contact with others who set their ambition on living outside of any obedience. This becomes an opportunity for the parents to consider the foundations of proper obedience anew and to seek ways of realizing them within the family circle. Out of their love for the children, which grants them their own life inasmuch as a child is capable of receiving it, they will build up the order of obedience. Through the felt love of the parents, and through it alone, can the children grasp something of obedience. Only thus will they desire to obey, not merely in order to be a pleasing child, but rather for the sake of something higher that they themselves cannot entirely understand, but that they accept as a law of their childhood existence. The obedience of the child can have a rebounding effect back upon the parents' relationship with each other and to their work and, indeed, even to their Church. From the family, a new sense can open for the ecclesial community, for the Word of the divine Father that he addresses to us in his obedient Son, a new sense of the Scripture and the Commandments.

Of course, the opposite path is just as accessible: from the living obedience of Christ to that within the Church; this living obedience then becomes the guideline of the family's common life and makes it into an efficacious cell by a lasting and joyful transmission of the law of the Church into the law of the family. The God-Man gives the highest and purest example that man serves his fellowman; this example works itself out in the most modest regions of the human community, where each person, through the obedience that is owed him, becomes for the other a permanent sermon that is impossible to miss.

The Apostolate in the World

The Christian, who often bears with difficulty the burden of both being conformed and having to conform himself to various orders in the world—it seems oppressive in its constancy and apparent pointlessness and often rouses the feeling that one lives in a prison—recognizes in faith the entirely differently configured structures of the Church's religious orders and the unity of this ecclesial order around the Lord as the head, who brings all order to the Father and lets the Holy Spirit blow through it. If the Christian in the world attempts to make a concept of this order, he will see the great lines, but also the small and the smallest branches, and therein, ultimately, also the place he himself has to occupy. This space has a double aspect. It is ordered to the Christian in question, set free for him; it waits for him. At the same time, however, it is the space that must be fulfilled, not only by the Christian's coming to possess it, but rather through the fulfillment of the claims that the Church places upon the Christian and that remain unresolved questions without his cooperation. He finds in this place a shelter; the Church, however, finds in the Christian an answer, if he is alive enough to let himself be asked and to want to answer.

The Christian in the world belongs just as much to the communion of saints as do the Christians in the states of priesthood and of religious orders. Every Christian must radiate, and if the apostolate in the state of the world takes on other forms than that in the state of the priestly life and religious life, so must it therefore not be any less lively. The

people whom Christ encountered were to the least
extent those who believed in him; many, however,
felt themselves to be addressed, disturbed, placed
in question; what they heard from him and what
they perceived about his way of life, they discussed
further, and they were, whether they wanted it or
not, permeated by his leaven and became themselves a kind of leaven; a part came to faith, a part
continued to act as a signal amid the unbelievers,
the indifferent, the doubting, the dissenters. Everyone who heard a sermon or saw a miracle returned
home with some barbed hook in his heart. Something had ripple effects in his behavior in family,
community, and nation. The Lord will pass on to
his Church this style of having an effect through
contagion, and it especially will be the laity's mode
of action in the world.

Of course, those who became true disciples also
received their tasks in the Church. The Church,
however, is not separated from the world; the
world breaks into her from every side. A perpet-
ual exchange between the world and the Church
is supposed to take place according to the will of
her Founder, and even *this* exchange has something
about it that is reminiscent of the inner-divine
exchange. The world belongs to the Father as the
Creator, and the Church belongs to the Son as
the Redeemer (although they hold all in common),
and the exchange takes place in the Holy Spirit. It

is a very distant, fumbling imitation: as a child tries to imitate what the father does and brings him his work so that he might improve it and therein recognize some work of his own, so do the believers bring their spiritual efforts, their attempts at an exchange to the divine exchange of love, so that God might work upon it further and complete what is for them unfinished.

In all of this lies, for the Christian in the world, once again, obedience. The Church is his home; she needs him, not only as her member, but rather because he is a Christian in the world, and by obeying his Christian life, he has to radiate that which is Christian into the world. But it also belongs to the Christian's obedience to call the world's attention to Christ through his existence because he is in the world and the world is created inwardly toward Christ. His existence as a Christian in the world is the interplay of a double obedience.

The sacraments are a special encounter between the Church and the world in which something worldly becomes the bearer of the Lord's grace. Thus, they are like a guiding thread for the Christian, and he must subordinate himself in a special obedience to the claim of their reality. Beside the sacraments, much in the Church is firmly regulated form, an imprinted word, which is not always understandable for everyone in its complete scope, but remains a regulation that can sometimes strike him severely. The whole Church thereby receives somehow the character of a great sacrament that would like to impress its holy form upon the matter of the entire world. Thus, in his obedience, the Christian in the world is taken into service for this process in an intensified sense.

The Relationship of the States

The person in the state of the counsels is constantly steered toward the Lord by the whole constitution of his life; he experiences in a certain immediacy that he has been created with an aim toward Christ. With the Christian in the state of the world, things are not so simple. He has interests, work, joys, and sufferings that belong to the world. He must make an effort to remember God again and again; even were he to go to Mass daily and receive Communion, he would still necessarily be distracted by his occupations. His thoughts are elsewhere. He also usually lives among people who hardly think about obedience and in many ways refuse it. Even if he tries to place his whole life under the sign of obedience and to do this in connection with like-minded people, the feeling of community would scarcely have for him as strong an effect as it would in religious life. It is as though the fullness and breadth of things that assail him are too great to be permanently gathered and offered to the Lord. Nevertheless, he must strive for this. And the Church counts on his collaboration. But despite goodwill, it will not be easy to keep always fully in mind those things that would be important for Christian radiance.

The secular priest, in virtue of his official role, sits nearer to the Christian in the world than the religious does. He is strongly shaped by his clerical milieu, however. He lives for the dispensation of the sacraments and preaching; the visible Church is his chief concern; he strives to lead the people of the world into the Church so that they find themselves at home there and fulfill an obedience that appears to them "natural". But perhaps he does not always give himself a sufficient account of what this "naturalness" means for the people of the world and how the Church appears from their perspective. Thus the same words often have different sounds in the mouths of each, and there is some distance and estrangement between them. A trace of such strangeness occurs again between all ecclesial states, not always as the product of tepidity or ill will, but rather as a sign of the tension that must obtain between the states, or if one looks more carefully, between the states in their entirety and the Church herself. The Church is indeed the narthex of eternity, the space in which Christ lives eucharistically and promises eternal life and the vision of the Father. And Christ experienced this tension himself on the earth as God and man. As man, he took on our ordinary conditions of life, and yet he was continually obedient to the Father in them—even unto death.

The Christians of the world feel this tension particularly intensely because it imposes itself on them again and again under new forms; they encounter it even where they do not expect it; now and then they rejoice to find it because it offers them new points of access for their faith and for their membership in the Church. Another place is revealed to which they may carry God, another place where they can sow seeds that will ripen into fruit. Fruit in the Church is always a sign of obedience fulfilled. God receives something and lets it ripen; God blesses a seed. And each ripened fruit bears in itself new seeds whose numbers grace alone determines, and which grace alone will let sprout, so that even the smallest obedience belongs to a great fruitfulness in the Church, and the layman may have the consciousness that, despite his deficiency and inadequacy, he partakes in this fruitfulness by living from it and again contributing to its liveliness.

8

Obedience in the
Life of the Counsels

Obedience in the Novitiate

A young person who considers the life of the counsels knows about the meaning of obedience from
the outset. Perhaps he is unable to present a clear
idea of it from without; he spies in it above all the
commitment to a community, that the order of
the day is extensively prescribed, and that his decisions depend upon a superior. He trusts that he has
the ability to be obedient. Already by his decision
to enter some community he wants to prove his
obedience. He prefers God's will to his own; he
gives his life to God in the context of an ecclesial
community. Behind this community, he sees the
Church as a whole; behind the Church, the Triune
God. He considers the mysteries of the life of Christ
from the perspective of obedience. In this way, he
comes upon love. Obedience and love coincide in
the Lord; he obeys out of love in order to show the

Father more love and in order to open for the world a sense of love. His love goes so far that it constantly denies itself in order to become aware of the love of one's fellowman and to foster it. In some way, the one entering the life of the counsels knows about all of this.

Experience in the life of the counsels then shows, however, that obedience has many faces, some of which are unexpected. Just what is now demanded one thought he would not have to face; precisely this he had not factored in. Indeed, it appeared to lie completely outside the field of obedience. Obedience turns out to be an attitude of each moment, a very narrow path along which there is just room for the present demand and nothing else. Everything one could imagine to lie left and right of the path already belongs to complete disobedience and, therefore, no longer to love.

The first place in which a novice can be trained in obedience is prayer. He prays in order to make the attempt to obey God. In this prayer, he quiets himself so that God can speak. He grows quiet in order to listen; he seeks what he will certainly find, that is, the love of God. He seeks out of obedience because it is now his duty to live in the unconditional love that he cannot receive from anyone but from God himself. Besides, there is everything that surrounds prayer: the order of the day, certain tasks, the interior approach to life. This approach, however, from the perspective of prayer, has above all the character of an obedience. The novice's day is scheduled down to the last moment. The novice is always prescribed something to do; even free time is prescribed as such. If prayer is prescribed, this is easy to understand; if something else is prescribed, it often seems incomprehensible. The question "why", however, is so much overtaken by obedience that it must remain unspoken wherever it is not one's task to question. The true answer to the question "why" is, ever anew, obedience itself. Sharp lines of obedience are drawn for sleeping, getting dressed, eating, recreation, and work, which are supposed to transform the person of the world into a religious. A free person becomes one who has chosen and who holds so firmly to his choice that he must continually reassert it. The great assent of the beginning somehow withdraws into the distance in order to make room for small, almost point-like assents. Commotion, hesitation, haste, and prolonged discussion can already count as a transgression of an imposed obedience. All of this is for the sake of making the person more supple for integration into the divine will. This will does not permanently reveal itself only in its greatness; it shows itself in the littleness and the pettiness of the superiors' will, in a more or less understood rule, and in the integration into common life. But the whole is the will of Christ, of God incarnate.

If one traces the lines through the life of the Lord only summarily, one will become aware of the great features of obedience. If one takes a single day, however—for example, one of the hidden, still, silent days in Nazareth—one will then see how his obedience is that of every moment, and how he gives every moment its inner content. The hiddenness as such obtains its countenance as something unforeseen. Such a day or moment sits apparently as something meaningless beside the great hidden countenance of the Lord on the Cross and is nevertheless meaningful because it is a preparation, a rehearsal created for the Cross that crowns all the little acts of obedience, gathering them into one.

The Rule and the Holy Spirit

Obedience often appears to Christians in the world as something that only arises in certain moments. It comes up, for example, when they encounter the precepts of the Church. Besides these, they appear to be more or less free to do what they please, to be able to align themselves, for example, according to the Augustinian phrase *ama et fac quod vis*[1] as the maxim of their life. If they take this seriously, however, they begin to observe that obedience, indeed, does not possess a sporadic character.

[1] "Love and do what you will."

In the state of the counsels, on the other hand, obedience is something so pronounced that it deliberately governs everything. The rule makes sure that the promise of obedience corresponds to a lasting demand. Did the Lord also have a rule? If one considers his life from the outside, it could appear more or less to depend upon his own discretion. Why did he spend thirty years in hiddenness and three years in action? Why does he do this and not that? Why does he go there rather than here? It is not completely evident to his family or to his disciples. Arguably, in speaking of his "Hour" that has not yet come, he shows that the Father commands the mysteries of his life that he does not know, and he makes no arrangements to come to know them. With respect to what is unknown, he remains in the dark, because the Father wills it. On the Cross, he gives his Spirit back to the Father and, indeed, in such a way that, from the perspective of the Cross, the obedience of his entire life will become visible. The Spirit of the Father was his rule to which he conformed his life. He was so obedient to this Spirit that the Spirit *was in him*, that not even for a moment did he distance himself from the Spirit but, much rather, left to him the whole rule of his life, not merely the rule of the great moments, when he did and proclaimed what was decisive, but also the rule of the small ones: the rule of those moments we cannot access or discover. By giving back to the

Spirit, the Son reveals the presence of this Spirit. He shows what his life has been all along. And all the words he has spoken, especially the words calling to discipleship, take on an enhanced significance from this perspective.

"Follow me", says the Lord, and this call is a word of the Word of the Father, spoken in obedience to the Father, guided by the Holy Spirit. If men choose a life of obedience and undertake it in the Son's discipleship, then it is clear to them that their body now belongs to the order, that they are sent where perhaps they do not want to go, while their spirit belongs to the Holy Spirit, who is embodied in the spirit of the order. Thus, they have to live continually under obedience to the Spirit, and this means the true discipleship of the Lord. It is the discipleship of every moment, which is manifest not only on great occasions, but rather in every detail unto the unseen and the moments when no one is present but God to perceive the effects of this obedience. As the life of the Lord was a sovereign act of love for the Father wherein men and the Father's entire creation are enclosed, so everything is included in the obedience of discipleship toward which the vow reaches: life in this state and in no other, under this rule and no other, in the readiness to be placed here in one's homeland or away in the missions, in the readiness also to live each little moment in the spirit of the rule. Most of

the little moments of such a life will hardly be outwardly distinct from the life of other men. But obedience transforms their value. They belong to the
Lord, who on earth placed himself entirely under
the rule of the Spirit, the strictest rule, because at
every moment it prescribed the completely fulfilled
dedication unto death, until the return of the fully
completed mission back to the Father.

Assimilation to the Rule

Each rule of an order is developed in the Spirit. It
is developed in a spirit of love and of obedience.
The founder or the first generation of a community work on it in prayer; there can also be external
causes that influence the formulations, but as far as
their core is concerned, the rule is, if the founding is
carried out in obedience to the Spirit, an expression
of this same Holy Spirit. And in the keeping of the
rule, one will experience what the Spirit intended
with the founding.

A founder knows about the necessity of a rule.
He knows also, however, that the rule is only poorly
followed. He knows that one always remains *beneath*
and lags behind the rule, that his devotion and his
obedience will never suffice to correspond to the
whole Holy Spirit of the rule in all his demands. If
Christ takes the Spirit as the rule, God stands in the
form of man before God the Spirit, God in the rule

stands before God in the exercise of the rule. Here, absolute correspondence obtains. The Son performs everything that the Spirit expects of him; and also the Spirit does everything that the Son expects of him. The Father, however, sees in this correspondence precisely what his will is. He never sees a deviation, a gap, a lagging behind.

It can happen that a religious, by way of exception, exaggerates certain points of his rule, that he lives, so to speak, *beyond* his rule, perhaps because the rule did not formulate this or that point sharply enough, or also because the one who is obeying understands and carries out the matter in an exaggerated way. Despite such occasional surpassing, everyone knows that he remains *beneath* the rule, that an essential gulf obtains between what is prescribed and what is carried out. Often, this gulf does not become visible in the initial wave of enthusiasm that characterizes the novitiate. One takes a perfect correspondence to be possible. But precisely the mirror of the rule lets one's weaknesses come to the fore; precisely this love for the rule makes the distance clear. It is the guideline, corrective, and ideal for which one strives.

The response to the rule is fundamentally an act of love. This act, as freely as it is performed, can for all that only be preserved by obedience in a living manner, indeed, can only thus be first performed. It is only sustained by the obedience of each moment.

Love cannot suddenly give way to indifference
or reluctance; it is of love's essence that it must
remain and desires to remain. Thus, obedience is
always already implicit within love. This obedience
is unfolded over time, and it is determined to the
last by the rule in all its details and implications.
The word of Christ: "Not my will, but yours be
done", is quickly said, but slowly done: the deed
fills his entire life. This life-deed is the complete
assimilation of the Son's will to the Father's will.
The will that is proclaimed in the rule of the religious order is an attempt to imitate this assimilation. However much the rule has its origin in the
Holy Spirit, so much is it also the work of a man
who knows about human weakness; as each individual religious knows, so too does the founder
know about the gulf that yawns between what is
prescribed and what is carried out. And thus there is
an aspect of the rule that appears adapted to human
weakness. Obedience is there, however, to close
this gulf and to *supersede* knowledge about the gap.
Obedience has an attractive power: it draws the one
obeying back into the rule. It enables him to understand the words of the rule suddenly anew and in a
different way: not as words that are adapted to him,
but rather as words to which he has to adapt himself. In obedience, he dares to identify himself with
the words of the rule without concerning himself
with the gap. With this daring is presupposed that

he really is capable of renouncing himself and of an elevation beyond himself. The spark of enthusiasm that is the source of love is also the spur of obedience. The same obedience, however, also has the ability to release tensions, entanglements, and inhibitions and to proclaim the Lord's satisfaction with the one obeying, to console him, to encourage him, and to elevate him. He is one of these little ones who come to the Lord and receive from his goodness. He is one of those to whom access to the Lord cannot be denied, one who knows the gate to the kingdom of heaven. In his obedience, he has a key that never fails, a consolation that always works, a help on which he can always count.

9

The Dangers of Obedience:
Its Boundaries

The Refusal of Responsibility

Whoever chooses God for the content of his life, whoever desires to see nothing else beside him (but rather everything only in him), makes one's choice for obedience in order to align himself as strictly as possible with the Son of God and his relationship to the Father. He wants to follow. He has a will that he desires to hand over; he desires, through an act of the will, which he understands to be an act of love, to place all his future acts of will at the Lord's disposal, so that no longer his will but, rather, the divine will may decide. Each act of will is supposed to be supplanted by an act of the love that is always becoming anew.

While he might ponder this and let his resolution ripen in prayer, he cannot overlook the consequences. He can perhaps know more or less accurately what he forsakes and have a premonition of what awaits him. But he can do no more than this. He makes a pledge in faith that the ever-present Lord will accomplish everything according to his holy will. But at the first decision, he would like to embrace the future in at least an open readiness, in such a way that no fundamental change would be necessary, that even the most extreme possibilities, which now he cannot see and therefore cannot name, would be included in the realm of which the Lord should be able to dispose. This extremity should be at least formally included so that it fundamentally belongs to the sacrificed good.

If the Son is obedient unto death, he assumes responsibility not only for his act of obedience, but also for his obedience's content. Obedience lets him face things with a new feature that has grown out of his decision: constant availability, and indeed, such a one that never lets his responsibility slacken. Through obedience, he does not at all become the Father's weak-willed tool. He has his will, through which he lets the will of the Father be done; he has his clear knowledge, with which he assumes responsibility for his obedience ever anew. This responsibility extends to the entire obedience promised to the Father, but also effectively to its present content, to that which is right now to be done in obedience. He does not assume things in a weak-willed manner; they are not neutral and lifeless for him, as though they would have the greatest significance for the Father, while he himself met them only accidentally, from a distance, without conviction as to the integrity and significance of his actions. He works his deeds with complete participation. Every encounter, every work belongs to his task and therefore has in itself something of the presence, vitality, and meaningfulness of the one who handed the task over to him, namely, the Father.

This example of the Lord shows that obedience to life's end may never become an indolent letting-happen. The Christian who desires to be obedient has to muster as much participation as possible for his work; in no way may he perform things indifferently, apathetically, or partially turned away. The things he does demand the opposite, namely, love and attention. Indifference would clearly be a weakness of faith. The Christian would err if he thought he had placed his will in another's hands in such a way that God could no longer demand from him either insight or interior cooperation. No, he commits his will into the hands of God and of his superior and of his order with the readiness to receive joyfully everything that is assigned to him and, furthermore, to perform it with the participation that the matter itself also demands.

God the Father created him with understanding, will, and a soul; God the Son redeemed him together with all of his abilities; thus, he may not despise the divine gifts and graces that have been doubly given

to him. To refuse human and Christian responsibility would be ingratitude to God. Whoever would
do this, would look upon obedience as a foreign
worldly power to which one delivers oneself up and
under whose spell one drifts impersonally without
interior commitment, deferring all responsibility
to his superior or God. Whoever thinks this way
proves that his obedience has died; by distancing
himself from his task, he distances himself from obedience itself.

To grow dull and lose one's personality is therefore a danger. Admittedly, acts of depersonalization
or self-renunciation *could* be demanded. From one
who is especially impatient and an activist it could
be demanded that he now should persist in being
completely tranquil and slow and patient. In a way
he is supposed to put on a different temperament in
order to show the validity of obedience. Another
must occupy a post that does not suit him or must
assume it because there is no one better available.
But also in such cases, it is always the person with
all his abilities who is requested; and even here we
see the difference between what is really demanded
and what is not demanded, between that which one
is supposed to offer and that which is actually left to
one's own responsibility or given back to him. Only
with this distinction will an obedience be worthy in
a way, however remote, to be compared with the
Lord's obedience.

The superior, however, who has to take the place of God in this relationship of obedience, must observe with clear vision what is going on in the one obeying. He must understand and discern. He cannot be content that a task has been completed in accordance with his instructions. He must also see *how* it was obeyed, how far the dedication of the whole person followed, how great the faithfulness and love were. In Christian obedience there may be no "as if". One may not do things as though one loved them; one must actually love them. Here, indeed, lies the deepest aspect of what obedience demands: the insertion of a living love where until now aversion, displeasure, and unfamiliarity reigned. Love interweaves obedience, bears it, and makes it become fruitful. True obedience is nothing but a fruit of love. Where love is no more to be found, obedience has *degenerated*. It can turn into its own negation.

Certainly, the superior's obedience and the subordinate's obedience do not need to meet at the exact same point every time in order to be valid. Materially, in a concrete situation, one could have grasped obedience differently from the other. There is, however, a continual encounter in love for God and in the love of God for his creatures. Here is the source; here, too, is the testimony. The testimony of the highest witness, of the Spirit, who causes the encounter, preserves both the superior and the subordinate, and from their love he begets a love worthy of the Spirit. From the seed he brings about a complete fruit, and from weakness he brings about the strength of unflagging discipleship.

Externalization: The Danger of the Religious Order

Old orders have their traditions; obedience is formed together with them, even if new tasks are set. In new communities, too, it should acquire a certain expression that secures, and sometimes clears out, its place between virginity and poverty. But because obedience is rooted in love, the features of its expression may never stiffen. Therefore, it may never withdraw into itself, but must remain in the harmony of the three vows in the unique commitment to the Lord that is given ever anew, that of the order as well as that of the individual.

It can happen that a religious remains in the beginning stage of the novitiate; he spent, so to speak, all his power at this level. As a novice, he thought he was already so familiar with all the mysteries of religious life that he ultimately took the path of lesser resistance to be obedience, although this is only its caricature. One can become accustomed to everything, and if something changes, he relents instead of obeying. One carries out everything with which he is tasked in a kind of sleepy repose or even a passive sullenness; he does not drift from the prescribed way, but he never does what is demanded, because the deed would require an authentic, personal commitment. One moves in a rut without interiorly confronting obedience, without assenting to it from the ultimate foundation of faith and love. Such indolence can erase the outlines of obedience until it is no longer recognizable. On his deathbed, such a religious must recognize his thoroughgoing disobedience, since his external deference had no roots. He confused the rutted track with the deep trails of obedience.

If God already took the effort to create each person differently from the others, he may also demand a response of personal obedience from each one: responsible planning, authentic acceptance, and commitment with one's whole person. The person can stumble, err, and at times fail; if his attitude of obedience is alive, however, he will catch himself. It is to this liveliness that the superior, to whom an account is given, must direct his attention. Only by way of exception may he content himself with the presentation of an exterior performance. Indeed, he himself needs a glimpse into the vitality of obedience in order to be able to be a superior. He needs it, in any case, in order, in the unifying prayer of his order, in the order's common will of discipleship, in the name of all who obey and of himself, who has to obey no less than the others, to present to God his area of responsibility and to have it be totally approved by God. So that an order's obedience may be visibly lively, its whole, which consists of countless little posts, must be able to be brought before God—like a thoroughly leavened dough. Everything that excludes, separates, encapsulates is deleterious to unity and dangerous also for the other members who would like to obey. The substance of the order wanes, becomes thin and brittle, and it can only be brought before God as something pasted together.

Because the one who obeys, or who at least strives for obedience, has promised to live as a member of a community, to figure as a point on a certain line, to act as one among many, every step that he takes aside from this, which is to say, not in love, is dangerous not only for him and his path of salvation, but also for the whole community. His illness is necessarily contagious. He brings the obedience of the order into arrears. The discipleship of Christ in this community is veiled, hidden both from itself and from those outside it. What the Lord demands from his own is no longer intelligible. Faith itself falters: not only if clear acts of disobedience occur; it also falters if obedience is carried out tepidly, lived falsely, or somehow caricatured. There is a language of obedience that is terse and in which every word bears significance. It says only what it must say, but it says this completely. If in this language room is no longer left for silence, if it is robbed of its power by embellishments and weakening paraphrases, it is as a language, as a mediator of commands, and as the acceptance of commands already alienated from the truth. Likewise, too, is it alienated from love and from obedience done. There is a humility of the superior like that of the subordinate that only flourishes in, and becomes fruitful through, true obedience. Indeed, it becomes fruitful until it no longer knows itself, until obedience becomes completely natural, until the permanent Yes really becomes the Lord's Yes to the Father, the Mother's Yes to the angel. Mary's Yes is the most concise word. But even the message of the angel, which already had the form of a command, was completely concise and transparent and said only as much as occurred in obedience.

The Finitude of Obedience

If the Son is obedient to the Father unto death, death can be grasped in worldly terms as a temporal boundary. As long as the Son lives in time, he obeys and his obedience appears to us to increase, because the Mount of Olives and the Cross are shown as the final levels before death and only this can put an end to the increase. If we understood these levels in a purely human, limited sense, the infinite significance of the work of redemption would be incomprehensible. But such limits do not exist for the Son at all because he also exercises in his human nature a divine obedience and lives as a Divine Person in what is unlimited and stands before the infinity of the Father. His earthly behavior is constantly open to this boundlessness, and even his obedience unto death does not come up against a temporal boundary that would necessarily put an end to it but, rather, finally pours out his interior infinity into dying and being dead.

The man who tries to follow is not God; he is finite. He knows that he is destined to die, but for him death is a boundary of humanity, set down because of sin. There are for him besides many other boundaries, for example, that of a human community, which may be just as religiously conditioned. Further, there are the boundaries within man himself: the weaknesses of the will, the deficiencies of understanding, failing powers. Some of these boundaries he has always known; others, he only becomes conscious of when he attempts unconditional discipleship. He experiences painfully that his love is not infinite; suddenly, it desires to go no farther, but claims for itself a right to understand and is thus far removed from true humility.

He will also, however, come up against boundaries that lie in what has been laid upon him. The rule is always absolute where it borders on the Spirit of Jesus, represents him unbroken, and hands him over to be imitated. But it will explain him in human words that analyze and interpret him. Thus, a casuistry of the words of the rule develops according to which the boundaries of obedience can be specified so and otherwise and over again. This excuses the one obeying to a certain degree, because it reckons from the outset with his strengths and weaknesses, his merits and failures. Also, the way in which the individual superior interprets the rule can change. The rule can be softened just by interpreting it. The salt goes stale. This softening is what harms obedience the most. One can make it so rubbery and malleable that the subordinate's will, and perhaps also the superior's, bounces off of it as though it really were made of rubber and not the substance of the Holy Spirit, hard and clear as crystal. From a stale obedience develops general tepidity, weariness, and boredom. As soon as one who obeys feels himself getting bored, he is somehow standing outside of love, unless the obedient one is occasionally tested, to see, for example, whether he can persevere in the same position—almost to the point of unconsciousness. But as the same prayer repeated countless times never becomes tiresome because it is in conversation with God, who can never bore, whose word is always new, even if it sounds exactly the same, as, therefore, the one praying never loses his time, so the one who obeys does not lose time by performing monotonous duties of the same kind if he is able to give to his action the fullness of prayer, that is, if he stands before God and—as one obeying among countless others—places the ultimate meaning of his actions in God. The Lord gives him the Holy Spirit in the form of the rule. It is a peculiar thought that the Lord did nothing outwardly for thirty years and that yet none of his days, none of his minutes, was superfluous: all were used in order to form together the fullness of his obedience in waiting and patience. Since the three wise men came to visit him and offer him useless— and yet, absolutely necessary—gifts, he was on his Mother's lap, a small, clumsy child, who could neither walk nor speak, and yet already in complete obedience. And as the nard was poured out upon his head, he was still the same, unchanged Obedient One. Another hour struck, but each striking hour was one of Yes-saying, of letting-be, always in a personal being-present, in the active acceptance of the Father's will. If an obedient person were close to slacking because of the monotony of his duties, which appeared to him incomprehensible and meaningless, he would have to recall those times in the life of Christ that have no visible meaning for us because this meaning was perfectly veiled in God, perhaps even remained veiled from the Son himself while he was on earth, as the consequence of his own obedience, which renounced every understanding that was not imparted to him by the Father.

Again we are threatened here by the danger of an interior turning away from the task. One still does what one is supposed to do but no longer goes along interiorly. And yet, the Lord was present with all of his powers in each of his actions. It is unthinkable that he, once he decided to preach or to pray, would have done so, for example, with the feeling: "I could surely just as well do something else." One can object: he was good. Or: he possessed his own will and could choose for himself. Or: he wanted to prove something to the Father and so carried out his own plan. These objections miss the mark. There is only the inexhaustible assent of Christ for whom obedience is so above everything that he always makes it into a new expression of his love. Even he appears to come up against many limitations. The rich young man goes away, the people and their leaders harden their hearts, Judas betrays him, Peter denies him three times ... Everything appears to demonstrate a limitation upon his obedience, for he has come to redeem the entire world. And so it appears as though he had to strive all the more in order to prevent betrayal and denial and turning away. But the limitations lie on the part of sinners, not with him. His obedience remains infinite, and the obstacles of the sinners become an occasion to wound him and to pour out his blood and his obedience for all: thus, no opposition can hinder his obedience.

The Christian, on the other hand, who obeys on earth, comes up against limitations within himself as well as with his fellowmen with whom he must live. If he is not able to break through the limitations in his fellowmen, then he experiences their freedom. If he cannot break through the limitations that lie within himself, he will have to learn about his own sinfulness and thereby measure the distance that separates him from the Lord.

10

Obedience between Earth and Heaven: The Saints

The Endowment of Obedience

In becoming human, the Son of God becomes one among us, but he remains God and lives in the vision of the Father. And he obeys him like a child. As a human child, he also obeys his Mother; at the age of twelve, however, he appears to break through the barriers of obedience: he must be within what is his Father's. Suddenly, one sees that he lives, not only on earth, but also in heaven. To the robber, he says: today you will be with me in paradise. He needs words and images of our daily life in order to elucidate heavenly existence, expressions that also transcend the realm of our experience and demand to be interpreted in faith: his earthly words direct us believers to what is promised us in heaven.

Thoughts that we understand are suddenly used to express things we do not understand. It is as though a melody were unfolded from a chord and

this were once more gathered back into the chord
in order to be unfolded once more from this, but in
a wholly different way. The chord is like a promise that, covertly and for us undetectably, contains
in itself the fulfillment. The harmony of the chord,
however, is not destroyed by the melody; one can
always trace the melody back to it in order to make
the fundamental meaning present. Or it is as if in the
course of a symphony with its familiar instruments,
all of a sudden, in an instant, completely unexpected
instruments were to come in; afterward, one waits
to see if they come once again, but there is no need
for it; everything has already been said that needed
to be said there. Thus do heavenly things unfold
from words of faith; thus does something heavenly
begin at one point to sound—with the twelve-year-
old [in the Temple], for example—and afterward
the world of faith can close once again.

So the Son has lowered himself to such an extent
that he obeys men, too, in a little, daily obedience.
The Mother tells him to do this or that, and he follows, because he is one among us. He will also do
it perfectly, because he is perfect; indeed, he will
do it as God, because he never ceases to be God.
One must expressly realize that he is God in order
not to overlook the divine meaning in even the
smallest activities that each of us could do.

But every example of the Lord's obedience has
an interpretation in the Church. He relates to the

Church in a living relationship of the bridegroom to the bride; he created it as a unity from his unity with the Father: as a likeness. The distance of this likeness as we see it before us from his heavenly archetype appears to us as enormously great, because we only judge as men and perceive even the Church only with respect to her humanity. We see the substance of her relationship to the Lord and of the Son to the Father only through the veil of faith. And if our faith grows weak, and the transparency almost completely fades away, we get caught entirely in the humanity of the Church and no longer understand how, for example, the sacraments are conduits of the divine life.

God the Father created men according to his likeness. God the Son formed the Church according to his relationship to the Father. To both, to men as well as to the Church in her humanity, the possibility of turning away is given. Man's turning away is not only known by Adam and the Old Testament; we know countless sinners and belong ourselves to their number, and it can become very difficult for us to recognize the likeness of God in sinful men, which nevertheless persists. Our judgment is not competent here; there is a truth above men, which stands above our judgment. The Second Adam is sinless, is God himself, and reflects the divine in everything he does. But he does not separate the divine from the human: in him we do not

see only a likeness of God; we see the Son of the
Father. He is also precisely so by obeying. And he
gives this divine-human obedience to his Church,
and she receives it in the perfect immaculateness of
the Bride. Where she speaks the perfect assent, her
face is glorious, by the power of the unity with the
Son in the Father and in the Spirit. And this unity
lives unbroken, indeed, it lives ever anew, even if
deeply veiled, in every dispensed sacrament. It is the
work of the Son, who supports the Church with
the glory of his obedience and his love.

Nevertheless, one who just now accepted the
Lord into his heart can commit grave sins; one
who is tasked with watching over the good of the
Church can be unfaithful; one who has to preach
the Word of God in the name of the Holy Spirit
can constantly place himself in the way as an obsta-
cle and mix his own word into the Word of God.
Thus, ever anew is the face of the Church veiled,
stained, and disfigured beyond recognition. Disobedience to what the Son willed is the cause of this
whole estrangement.

This estrangement is always only possible for
the individual member of the Church. The individual lets his own sinfulness be seen, but because
sinners associate closely with other sinners, they
constitute, as it were, a wall behind which the face
of the immaculate Bride disappears. But there are
also the saints, and they direct their attention to

God. They see God, not only occasionally in their visions—for God is *in himself* always visible—they also have a way of considering the Church as a site of the manifestation of God, and they witness to the incorruptibility of the true Bride of Christ. The way in which they give this witness lies first of all in their obedience. It lives from what the Lord himself deployed by endowing the Bride with his obedience, by the power of which he is one with the Father and which binds him perpetually to the Spirit and keeps him in communion with him. Endowed obedience runs visibly through the hierarchy, even through religious orders, and through every affiliation to the Church; it attains its particular intensity in the obedience of the saints. As a whole, it is like a tree branching out broadly: the outer branches can dry out and break; the tree lives resiliently from the Lord's obedience. Much that appears to be dead has life hidden within itself, and it often does not take much for a branch to sprout again. The sap in every branch, however, is obedience, which corresponds to the innermost principle of life: the obedience that unites the Son with the Father.

Three Saints

The Little Thérèse walks her little way, makes her little sacrifices in a strict obedience, and directs her novices in the same direction: she moves in a

space that is marked out. She exerts her spirit to
carry out the best possible action in the smallest
space, but at the same time she opens this spirit
completely to God; she gives herself to the infinite
God in prayer and contemplation and desires to
know nothing other than the infinite love of God.

In this tension, the little Thérèse is like a model
of general human existence: contained within
a strict obedience on earth, but open to heaven
without limit. And thus is it possible to contain
the infinite within the little nutshell of obedience.
As through a narrowing funnel, heavenly love is
channeled to the little place where a rule is fulfilled
as exactly as possible, where, while living in the
world, something prescribed is carried out as well
as possible; whatever is done in this way will not
only satisfy the earthly superior or what has been
prescribed, but just as much the Triune God. Perfection can find room within the smallest detail,
if no turning away, resistance, or egoism is to be
found in one's conduct.

Thérèse, caught for a long time in a sort of night,
does not see what she does. She may not walk any
path where there is fruit to pick. God only desires
to see her fidelity. And this fidelity permanently
cracks open her soul, so that all of heaven can participate in her obedience; eternal life can participate in her earthly life. And the Son, who keeps
the rule of the Holy Spirit, guarantees that she

keeps her vows; he keeps them together with her; he gives her the power to hold out until the end, even the final power during her illness. She offers the cloister an image of little obedience; to heaven, however, she offers a likeness of heavenly obedience. She is capable of every expansion, because she refuses none. The Lord expands her limitations outward, so that they do not collapse in upon each other. Up to the last moment, he will guide her, and she will not stop loving him obediently.

John of the Cross walks the path of obedience in the difficulty of a complete night. He walks in the hopelessness and despair of a blindness that gropes onward while his hands find nothing that he can grasp or with which he can steady himself. Nevertheless, there remains what he lives: perfect obedience. Obedience amid persecution, amid slander, amid all the temptations that come from without, which race to knock him out of the path he has embarked upon and make him forget divine obedience in favor of a false obedience. This is obedience quite near to the Cross, knowing full well about the darkness to which he must assent. John remains steadfast in it; he has a faith in which obedience is completely veiled. The night of faith is perfect. In it, the smallest obedience that is performed can no longer be seen. John cannot perceive the fruits of his labor, of his prayer, of his suffering. Even if ultimately he is freed from the darkest night, he does not see what he has accomplished. He rejoices over what is given to him in a much easier obedience and more visible love; but he does not reflect upon the fruitfulness of the terrible night he has undergone. God needs this obedience of the night in order to bring his world, his Church, to life; but he alone measures its fruit.

Ignatius translates into his rules of obedience his own interior knowledge and experience. His demands of obedience are born from pain. From him, too, are the fruits continuously withheld so that they may be applied to the work and transformed into new seed. He may not enjoy anything. He knows that the path he opens up and illuminates will be fruitful in the Church, but he is not allowed to know that his own path belongs to the fruit, that his own word is God's Word interpreted, or that the whole fruit shall come forth from his own obedience. His obedience is not only marked by the fact that he submits to the Church's will and to the letter of his rule, but rather God gives it the character of a permanent vocation. He often sees things that at first he does not understand, that then accompany him in some form and that he must bear patiently, and only later does it become clear to him what the *content* of that form was that at first he had to take along obediently only as such. Thus, his obedience takes again and again the form of a *patience*, a permitting, a not being permitted to seize, which runs totally contrary to his temperament. It is surely for Ignatius one of the most difficult things that he must continually wait in obedience, and that he only ever in this way learns the kind of obedience that he has to give his order. He learns this form bit by bit, in a flexibility that is not allowed to stiffen, but that continually draws out of him the last bit of love and patience. Love and patience are thus sources of his obedience, even where he has already become most obedient and no longer thinks any more of doing anything other than the will of God. Even then he is still continually tested. And it is no discreet, imperceptible test, but rather something virulent that consumes him, that has and must have the ability to disturb him and place him ever anew at the beginning. This obedience is not only one that has him embrace certain tasks, that imposes certain forms of prayer upon him, or that prompts him to make certain utterances; it is an obedience that weaves him into the ultimate mysteries of prayer: his prayer is accompanied by things of God that make even conversation with God appear strange to him. This strangeness is not avoidance but, rather, an excessive demand. This excessive demand comes to light everywhere in his life. He is never allowed to rest. He is also drawn to this obedience by the fact that he is often only permitted to proceed extremely slowly: he reads many measurements and lets others read them in order to gain clarity somewhere and reach a decision. God proceeds with him as though he were another, as though his powers of perception, his understanding, his prayer were not to be used as they are. Precisely because he is himself *thus* must he bear the *other*. Out of this tolerance, there awakens new love, and from this, new obedience: obedience in the strictest form. In such a way must he learn to build up for those who will follow a supply from which they will draw without themselves being conscious that precisely what they considered a more or less normal observance of the Ignatian rule possessed for him such urgency and actuality— that every letter of his rule, every characteristic of obedience had to be purchased by him so dearly. God just did not want to offer him a cheap deal.

11

Obedience as Love

Participation in the Trinitarian Integration

It is difficult for us to touch upon the things of God
with our words and concepts because of the infinite
distance that obtains between God and his creatures.
We feel as men, love as men, and listen as men, and
everything that is ours is, on the one hand, personal
and corresponds to our predisposition and, on the
other, is social and conditioned by the community.
The community, however, is only held together by
human nature as such, without letting a single normal type receive the emphasis out of the fullness of
the variety. No human word—only the Word that
was in the beginning with God—is the singularly
true; and this word of an individual can be grasped
and interpreted by the other in an infinite number
of ways. Even if we speak in a small community
that gets along well, we give our word a personal
tone and content so that we might be the only ones
able to understand completely how we mean it.

The others understand according to their point of view at closer or farther distances. Thus, humanity in itself has no binding center; its center lies above itself in the Son.

If, however, at the creation of the world the Father ordered all things toward the Son, then the Son is present in the world everywhere as the goal. The world is an act of God that is carried out in a dialogue between the Father and the Son, and the Spirit, who hovers over the waters, is like the presence of this dialogue in the world. The presence of the Son and of the Spirit at the paternal creating foreshadows how immeasurable the divine love can be that is fulfilled in this eternal dialogue; it foreshadows, too, how immeasurable is the mystery in God for which we might need the name obedience: the perfect integration, the perfect, loving being-in-accord of God with God.

And creation is God's self-communication. The Father, who creates the world, does not in so doing withdraw himself into an inaccessible realm; his act is not only the expression of his love for the Son and for the Spirit—it is also thoroughly the expression of his love for the created world. God loves what he creates, and the presence of the Son and of the Spirit bears witness of this love to the world. Those who are witnesses of the divine *creation* testify to that creation that it is *divine* and originates in God and in love; they testify in the same act also to

God that the divine love bears witness to itself in the world. Even this bearing witness of God to the world and to God is the expression of obedience in which there is never a gap, an area of friction, roughness, or the possibility of misunderstanding. It is completely divine integration.

God invites us, his creatures, to participate in his seamless love. And because we threaten to fall away through sin, he gives us his Son in order to lift us back up. He gives him to us in the form of a man. But we cannot for a moment separate this Son from the Fatherly love or from the Triune love. In the Son we understand: God gives us his love in order to bring us back home to love. But the way he adopts usually is not pleasing to us. Thus we begin to argue with God—indeed, we have been arguing since the conversation with the Serpent in paradise. We give expression to our astonishment. If God earnestly meant to bring us back home, would he not have to speak with us more clearly, engage with us more effectively, make us offers that we could more easily accept, and provide things that better correspond to our human nature? But God, who becomes man in order to save us, cannot renounce thereby the nobility of his divinity. It is the most extreme thing that can be asked of him: that he consider us his fellowmen, bear for us the Cross, and die. We sinners have lost all refinement, and so we cannot comprehend the nobility of love that is not ours. We are those who are comprehended and would always like to be those who comprehend. Because this does not work, we constantly show ourselves unworthy of the divine love.

We cannot, however, content ourselves all our lives with the observation that God surely intended us not to understand his deeds and measure up to him, that our love is incapable of taking a form that would enable it to hold its own before the love of God. In order to help us beyond this despairing resignation, God gives us obedience as a valid expression of love. He shows us from the creation of the world the integration of God in God and invites us likewise to integrate ourselves. If we imagine love as obedience, we will understand—at least conceptually—more about love. We can understand obedience from the contrast between Yes and No; we see the assent as the opposite pole of rejection. Between the two there is no middle. There is no place where the feeling of accomplishment could wash over us or where we could find a synthesis of Yes and No. There is, however, not only in major situations but at every moment, the ladder of obedience to ascend higher, as a means, if not to understand, at least to be understood, and to understand this being-understood. Obedience is our integration into the encompassing love that we have recognized as the "being at one another's disposal". Thus it can indicate to us an abiding access to God. In order that we might be sure of this way, God gives us his Son, who sets for us the example of his integration with the Father in human obedience. In the imitation of the Son, we walk, almost without stumbling, through the door that leads to the Father.

Obedience in the Son's Integration

The men of the Old Testament received the law from Moses; it showed what offended God, what sin is, and how to avoid sin. The exposure of sin and the prohibition against it corresponded to the law of righteousness. The Father's love was still not therein fully revealed. Finite actions of men were measured: I have or have not done this or that.

The birth of the Son brings a change. The Word, which was in the beginning with God, is given to us and lives among us. His message is God's Word to us, is God himself. Wherever we hear the Word of God in the Son, however, and pass it on, we are occupied with the Word's obedience, the obedience of the Son to the Father, and have a share in the Word's being. For we may use what belongs to him. And God gives us his Word unbroken, unified, laden with all the significance that it has for God, as the Son, whom he himself has with him as his Word. And the Word also remains obedient to the Father as something vocalized: there is no weakening of the Word; on its path through the world, it does not gradually diverge from the Father. What the Son says, he is. In this sense, he is the truth. He also does not walk the path of perfection along which levels would be recognizable as farther from or nearer to the goal. He stands always in the same distance of the Son from the Father and thereby always in the same nearness to him. In his earthly life, no progress in this respect can be ascertained. He does not grow slowly into obedience. He remains God before God, the Son before the Father, man before the Triune God. Consequently, every word he utters is to be taken absolutely. It is in this absoluteness that obedience lies. And since the Word is issued to us, it *makes* us obedient, integrates us into his providence. It transforms us, gives us the gift of grace, and lets us live within it. And only if the Word is hidden by our sins does it become a lie within us. With the Lord, it is always a definitive testimony.

But God always remains God to such an extent that his Word, whether as a testimony or as obedience, is always only love. The whole relationship is love; everything is an exchange of love. And the exchange of Triune Love demands of us that the meaning and mode of our participation in God should be love. It demands that every action we do for God or for our fellowman should be an action of obedient love. We must be as obedient as the child who shows his whole love by bringing the one he loves most to his mother, and by seeing in this bringing the demand of love, indeed, by being more obedient to this demand than to the felt love itself. In this way, he acts out of pure love, without intervening thoughts, without reflecting, simply in order to be love, simply to give back what he has received, in his childlike, undeveloped, and yet perfectly loving manner. Whatever the child has, he brings to his mother. Whatever the child does, he does it somehow for the mother. He does not yet possess understanding and powers of consideration, but has only this love for his mother, this recognition of the mother, this will to act in accord with her.

In the conformity of adults to God lies the same obedient love. And if love does not make any considerations, it also does not need to number its fruits or pile its sheaves. Love brings everything back to God. It brings what can be counted and what cannot be counted, its own concerns and those of others, and lastly the unknown concerns of all. But when carried to God, a concern always has a form: it wants to correspond. What we bring in prayer to God is like a heap of jumbled stalks that together do not yet make up a harvest. Through our prayer, they should come to rest in such a way that God can use them, in such a way that conforms to God. And the more that people pray and do so obediently, the more correct becomes the world's response to God.

Obedience preserves a presence in the Church and, by obeying the Church, grows richer. It becomes a barn where the collected goods are found in the form of a treasury of prayer into which God can continuously reach in order to use what is at hand as he needs and desires it. The prayer of the one who obeys is the face of his obedience before God, and it passes over into the face of all whom the Son has come to redeem and, finally, into the face of the love of the Son, of his sacrifice, his Cross; but it is also the face of his years of childhood, of his love for his own Mother; something of his work is present there, and this too passes over into the face of the Lord's childhood, his love for Mary, his work, and his vision of the Father. This is not seen by the individual Christian, but God knows what the Son is: the Son knows his own, and the Father knows who belongs to the Son.

The Sacraments

The Christian sacraments signify our absolute bond to the Word of the Lord. This Word becomes an act, an act within us. God has become flesh, has wrought the most concrete, visible deeds among us and given them to us. Their content is divine—on the Cross the whole divine love squanders itself—but their form is human: we see how God suffers as a man, and his blood pours forth in order to wash away our sins. This concreteness of the invisible enters into the sacraments.

Each sacrament takes its substance from the Son's Incarnation. Each is poured out for us in more than one respect; there is always more within than we can grasp, but there is also always more demanded of us by the sacrament than we can perform—indeed, more than we can understand. In the sacrament, the incomprehensible more or less takes on a concrete form before us, because the sacrament as such already signifies a bond that is located in obedience: in the Lord's obedience to the Father. Somehow the Father shares with us at each reception of a sacrament something of the Son's concrete obedience. Receiving the Son, we are obedient to him and to the Church, bound to a new freedom, to the freedom of man in the Church, but also bound to the Lord and his obedience, and in that respect lastly also to our own emerging obedience.

We come to confession. We bear a certain weight of guilt and recognition of guilt, and out of an obedience we desire to confess this. When, however, we have received absolution, we are in the Spirit of a new obedience. We have received more from the Lord's obedience through a tremendous concretization of his Word within us and in the Church. We know that something happened that is much more eventful than our preceding confession and our readiness: something so concrete that it only finds a point of comparison in the Incarnation itself. From his Incarnation, the Lord gave us through absolution a new obedience, and it must be put into practice in our future life. For this purpose is it at our disposal, not in the weak form in which we are accustomed to give obedience, but rather in the strong, inexorable form that the Lord himself gives: a total, all-encompassing act. In daily life, we will tarnish this act once more, weaken it, forget it, and put it on the shelf. But perhaps we declare that we are ready to accept the obedience of the Lord, who now lives within us (although we can never portray him clearly enough), as something binding for a whole life—as something that expresses itself not only in our religious knowledge, but rather must also express itself in prayer and in our works. A new element is drawn into our attitude, one that we do not determine but that determines us; it is something given from beyond that draws us out of ourselves.

The Lord desires to live among the faithful in the communion of saints and to stand together with them before the Father. Rising, he abandoned the loneliness of the Cross. The sacraments should make us companions in knowledge and in bearing burdens; they should empower us to be present together before the Father. The Father sees the Son together with his own and recognizes them, as he does the Son, by their obedience to his call and word.

Accordingly, a Christian in the world, in an order, or wherever he may be, must be something radiant, a ray of the Lord who radiates among us. Whoever in the Church remains far from the sacraments would fail to receive, if not completely reject, some of the radiating presence of the Lord. The sacrament mediates something that can hardly be expressed in words, something that is so much a presence that it is only expressed by presence. But because it is the presence of the Lord within us, it is the presence of his obedience within us, and therefore it effects—despite our more or less strident opposition—our assent to his obedience.

The Liturgical Year

The Lord joins the celebration of the wedding in Cana. He does so in obedience to the Father and at the invitation of the people, who apparently cherish him, though they are not aware of his power. In the course of the celebration, there is suddenly the miracle, and the celebration becomes a celebration of the Lord and his Mother; the customary human celebration becomes a singularly divine celebration in which something of the glory of God is manifest. This glory is revealed by the emergence of the Son's role, and even in such a way that all receive their share of the miracle and are raised up from this festive mood into the super-festive through what the Lord does out of obedience and love. The barriers fall away; the standards are broken; the miracle lies there overtly in the setting of this celebration. It is a kind of demonstration: it brings the Lord into the light; it is at once a joyful invitation to his feast, to which all are invited in order to quench their thirst and lift their spirits. But one understands: all of this is only a hint of that feast which is much greater than any image or earthly miracle can express.

Christians celebrate feasts: in the space of the Church, at home in the spirit of the Church, wherever the festive season finds them. And they, too, invite the Lord to partake in their celebration as did the people of Cana. It is for them miracle enough that the miracle *par excellence*, the God become man, desires to be among them. Wherever he lingers, he transforms what is ordinary into the hopefulness of a believing obedience, a tepid love into a burning one. By this is his presence and his glory recognized. It belongs to his mission, indeed, to his essence, to transform our water into wine, our weakness into power, into an imitative, obedient faith that he himself can shape.

The feasts of the liturgical year repeat: again and again there is a First Communion, a wedding, or an ordination. And each of these feasts is unique through the Lord's manifestation. But in order for there to be a feast of the Lord, our obedience is required. It is not possible to skip Christmas or Easter this year in order to celebrate it next year doubly or in a way we would find more suitable. Obedience demands that we celebrate God's festivals. And indeed, it demands we celebrate them as joyful and exuberant feasts whose substance should please us and which should also overflow into our obedience. Celebrations quash barriers and bridge abysses. We may celebrate it out of God's joy. We do not need to look back scrupulously at our half-measures, nor do we have to celebrate as grumpy sinners; in obedience, we may partake in the extravagance of God's joy. The Lord does not allow the celebration of Easter to be overshadowed by the Cross. He celebrates his feast close to the Father and in his joy, in unity with him, and the Holy Spirit is the organizer of the festival. As such, he also blows through the Church across all the centuries, so that we may obediently submit to his Spirit and rejoice with God. To worry about yesterday or tomorrow is not allowed. One celebrates in imitation of him who left everything. One celebrates in the communion of saints, who hold everything in common. One carries his joys to the Lord and no less to his neighbor.

In this obediential joy, the commands of the Lord are fulfilled. They derive from this joy, and they flow back into it. And the celebration does not even depend upon which notions we associate with it, if only we have directed our gaze toward the Lord, who is the Great Reveler and who desires to carry home to the Father in the Holy Spirit all the joys of creation.